I0102040

WHATEVER HAPPENED TO COMMUNITY MENTAL HEALTH?

A retrospective set in Baltimore's inner city
and a call for a reassessment of mental health.

WHATEVER HAPPENED TO COMMUNITY MENTAL HEALTH?

A retrospective set in Baltimore's inner city
and a call for a reassessment of mental health.

Roger B. Burt, Ph.D.

Bivens & Jensen Publishing LLC

Whatever Happened to Community Mental Health?

A retrospective set in Baltimore's inner city
and a call for a reassessment of mental health.

Copyright © 2010 by Roger B. Burt, Ph.D. All rights reserved.

No part of this book may be reproduced or transmitted in any form or by any
means, electronic or mechanical, including photocopying, recording, or by any
information storage and retrieval system without permission in writing from the
publisher, except by a reviewer, who may quote and reprint brief passages in a
review.

Published by: Bivens & Jensen Publishing LLC

ISBN: 0977018385
ISBN13: 978-0-9770183-8-3

Published in the United States of America.
First Publication: April 2010

Contents

CHAPTER 3 Consultation to Community Agencies

Chapter 4 Functions and Problems of Professionals

Contents

Chapter 5 Administrative and Organizational Issues

Chapter 6 Advisory Boards

Chapter 7 Employing Residents of the Community

Chapter 8 Other Applications of the Service Model

Contents

Chapter 9 Unhealthy Health Politics

Chapter 10 Was Community Mental Health a Failure?

Chapter 11 the Mental Health Challenge today

This book is dedicated to the proud yet beleaguered people of the inner city of Baltimore. In our efforts to serve them, they were our teachers and guides.

Chapter I
Background and Contextual Issues

CONTEXT

In 1967 the community mental health movement was just beginning. After all my years in school, the last thing I wanted was an academic position. My final orals for my Ph.D. at Duke University were scheduled for the fall and in the spring I set out on a serious job search. The country was in the throes of major reforms. Civil rights workers were murdered in Mississippi, conflicts over social rights and enfranchise-ment spilled onto the streets, a bold poverty program had begun, and the media were serving up stories about "sex, drugs and rock 'n' roll". I could not wait to get out of the library and dive into the grand adventure that was unfolding before me.

HOW THIS BOOK CAME TO BE

One of the very first community mental health programs in the country was in Baltimore and they were just beginning to hire for a program administered by the University of Maryland. I took a flight to Baltimore arriving at what then was little Friendship Airport, the baby form of today's Baltimore-Washington International Airport. Carl Thistel, the lead community organizer (and the only one of them then on staff) met me at the airport. He whisked me away in his VW Beetle and nonstop regaled me with the history of Baltimore including the composition of the villages which made up an aging city badly in need of renewal. Within a half hour, simply by his enthusiasm and torrent of words, he had sold me on the job - if they would have me.

My first interview was with the voluble, enthusiastic Japanese-American direc-tor who further whetted my appetite for working in the program. After him I went to see the head of psychology at the University of Maryland Psychiatric Institute. We began talking and he promptly fell asleep. Patiently I waited for his nap to end, thanked him for his time, as if we had had a good conversation, and left. His nap turned out to be symbolic of the amount of investment the University had in the Program. It did not matter. How could I possibly turn down the chance to tramp grimy streets, climb urine-soaked stairs in the projects, and visit apartments where sitting on the sofa seemed a health risk? It was the perfect job for the son of an eminent surgeon who grew up in Scarsdale.

As it turned out, they wanted me, and so began my adventure. I could not know that my job would be as much community organizer as clinical psychologist. The experience shattered my remaining illusions about my profession and related mental health professions. It also was a "growth experience" that was totally unanticipated. We learned things we could not have considered necessary for a mental health professional to know. While the setting was inner city poverty, years later we could see the applicability of what was learned went well beyond that setting.

What follows is the story of young professionals in the inner city during a renowned period of national struggle. It is not intended as a scholarly exercise with a compilation of literature. It is variously a personal story, a comment on broad-based naivete, an appraisal of the community mental health movement, or a statement of what was learned and what could be applied to other settings. At the end I will share some views on how we might proceed at the dawn of another reform movement.

COMMUNITY MENTAL HEALTH AS A MOVEMENT

Beginning with the vigorous activity of reformers such as Dorothea Dix in the middle of the nineteenth century, the United States has seen a series of reforms in the treatment of the mentally ill. The reforms were typically a function of both humanistic concerns and advances in knowledge and conception that permitted needed changes.

Community mental health was a part of a wave of reform following World War II and coincided with a broader reform movement. Bold promises were made consistent with the climate of optimism.

The principles on which it was based were hardly new, and early in the twentieth century Dr. Adolph Meyer called for clinics offering an emphasis on service to the patient, management of the whole patient, and a preventive orientation.

The movement in the sixties can be traced directly to a 1955 Act of Congress that created the Joint Commission on Mental Illness and Health. This body undertook an extensive study of mental health needs and treatment modalities. Its report in turn led to the first presidential message on mental health and, in 1963, the

2

authorization by Congress of $150 million for a three-year period. The programs were based on the belief that the citizens of this country required comprehensive, continuous, and humane treatment without regard to their ability to pay.

In retrospect it is hard not to view the whole effort as naive, given our ongoing struggles to reform health care, which have been defeated again and again by special interests (read "private enterprise"). But, as we shall see, there were many other factors operating to influence the movement. It was a time when we actually believed that we could end poverty but were unable to end a war.

And yet, on the streets of Baltimore success was found, if only for fleeting moments. But there was a window to the future.

THE ORIGIN, PURPOSE AND ORGANIZATION OF THE PROGRAM

Since the concept of this book involves having both a story and a perspective, it is necessary to deal with the mundane matters of how things worked and were funded. As a staff we thought we did not care, because we had come to do a job, but soon we found ourselves mired in politics of all varieties. Try not to fall asleep.

The money created a program called the Inner City Community Mental Health Program (hereafter the Program) and the money came largely from grants from the National Institute of Mental Health (NIMH). The money flowed to the State of Maryland (hereafter the State) and then to the administrative unit, the University of Maryland (hereafter the University). The purpose of the Program was simple. By law it was required to deliver the five essential services of outpatient, inpatient, consultation and education, emergency, and day care. Easier said than done.

The State, which had cooperated with the University in developing the grant, gave over the administration of the Program to the University. This institution had hired one staff member to help write the grant and, thus, it was understood early on that the University would have a major part to play in the Program.

There were some powerful reasons for the University to administer the Program. Although there was supposed to be an emphasis on service, the University had the capacity to build in training and research components for a program on its doorstep. Because this was a bold, new venture, research and evaluation concerning its development were important. In addition, given that physical health care was also a major problem, an affiliation with a medical school was logical. It was a nice rationale and totally devoid of effective implementation.

Whatever Happened to Community Mental Health?

Thus, early on the University took administrative control and related to the State and the NIMH with an accountability system that was most obvious to the staff only during site visits, when the Program was visited by State and Federal officials. Site visits were a source of great anxiety and distress for the administrators of the Program and the University.

At times staff positions had been given to people who did not actually work in the Program. Described services were often little like they were portrayed. Those of us who worked in the trenches, as it were, were expected to be loyal soldiers. We were realistic enough to know that if we were not "loyal" it could have serous consequences for us and the people we were serving.

Even worse, the people making the site visits were often romantics who were strikingly naive. And so we suffered long lectures from people we regarded as totally "clueless". Over time we lost all respect for our "betters" and the elders we were supposed to revere in our professions. We were mostly in our twenties and were treated like upstart children. We, in return, felt most of the senior staff supposedly overseeing us were hopelessly out of touch with the reality of the service delivery. In addition we often saw them as venal, self serving, status oriented and most interested in protecting turf. At least that is how it looked to those of us who were dedicated to developing a viable system of services suited to the population of the area.

Later, when there was conflict about services and considerable staff unrest (to put it mildly) over the relationship with the University, the administration was given over to the State, and, at least temporarily, the University took a secondary role.

At the time of my arrival, the most obvious place to begin giving service was with outpatient services. Over time the other four required components came into being. There came to be a 15-bed inpatient unit in the Psychiatric Institute, a day care program, an emergency service, and consultation and education services. The central administrative unit existed in offices in the Psychiatric Institute. Eventually there were three outpatient satellite centers. The vast majority of direct services were given in those centers and they set the tone of the program.

Initially the director of the program served both as head of clinical services and administrative services. As the program matured and became more complex it was clear that there needed to be a separate administrator. The fact of the matter was that clinicians were generally taught nothing about administration or money matters. Also in the central office were the director of psychiatric services, the director of children's services and the community planner or community organizer. The latter

4

person tried to be absent from those offices as much as possible because of the climate, which our staff thought was out of touch with reality. Street reality conflicted with bureaucratic reality which conflicted with academic reality. Street reality was our reality.

The directors of the outpatient satellite centers took charge of consultation and education activities. The director of the inpatient service was in charge of inpatient services and day care activities. The emergency service had only what we would now call a virtual location, in that a duty roster was managed by an executive secretary. Over time each service became more structured.

The service or "catchment" area was a matter of routine planning in such programs. The design was for 200,000 people in a defined area. For obvious reasons the Program could not serve the entire city of Baltimore. At the outset the catchment area included 100,000 people.

PROGRAM PROBLEMS

Although every staff has its problems, the staff generally did not constitute the source of major problems, at least from our viewpoint. Other people might have disagreed. This new endeavor attracted dedicated "can do" types of people. There was never a problem getting things done or having people take on new and challenging opportunities. The Program attracted very special people and the first director was good at luring them. The staff was composed of willing workers who tended to be activists but were generally moderate. There were some immoderate, even radical, people, but they were generally contained by a service-oriented staff.

In the beginning it was apparent that University personnel had a very different view from that of the "line" staff. It seemed that the ideals of the community mental health movement were not shared by University administrators. Clearly staffing money and traditional training opportunities along with the planned multimillion-dollar central building were the attractions for them. Our staff was a constant bone in their throats.

My graduate training had taken place at Duke University where the Department of Psychology was next door to the Medical School. We spent a lot of time there, and it was there that I did my internship. The Department of Psychology was an open-door kind of place where we had easy access to our professors. We listened to them and they listened to us. The Medical School was on another planet. Residents were not permitted to make diagnoses, and the medical students were relentlessly

5

"hazed". Their treatment in the Department of Psychiatry was even worse. When psychology interns presented the findings from their evaluations (battery of tests) they were used to embarrass both the medical students and the residents. After a six-week rotation the medical students left gratefully and surely never wanted anything to do with mental health again.

The regime at the University of Maryland was little different. Medical students were given brief rotations to do "psychotherapy" with inner city residents. The mentally ill and the suffering were subjected to a series of therapists on six-week rotations. They were not only inexperienced but were not given a proper orientation to the management of their "patients".

The University looked at our clinics greedily. There was just one problem. The staff would have nothing to do with bringing in medical students for six-week rotations. Incredibly this staff of "kids" said a polite and firm "no". We gained enmity by generally taking stands at odds with University goals. Our only real plus was that we helped them hide their misdeeds when it came time for site visits. It was in our interest as well to avoid a seriously embarrassing revelation that might do harm to the funding of the Program.

The University was not interested in changing its approaches or making a commitment to the poor and disadvantaged population surrounding the campus. We learned that the faculty had been deeply divided about whether to enter the field of community mental health at all. And there we were, caught between the crossed swords of a service-oriented State and a training-oriented University. But nirvana was not achieved when the State later assumed administrative control. Our new bosses sat in distant offices and, we felt, were inclined toward the most pedestrian and traditional services.

Another problem with which the staff had to contend related to basic inadequacies in the original staffing grant. It was inconceivable how some of the errors could have been made. Probably the most glaring example was in the conception of the emergency service, for which the grant mandated two full-time individuals to run a 24/7 service. It was no wonder that these potentially overburdened individuals were immediately dispatched to outpatient clinics and that the entire staff was placed on a rotating duty roster to provide emergency services. Meetings about this problem often included angry exchanges. We were all too aware that emergency calls could come during busy morning walk-in clinics or late at night. But we participated in site visits in which we all pretended to have a smoothly operating service and to be in perfect harmony. It was invariably a sixties love feast.

Of course, during site visits the real danger was that we might not know what sleight of hand had been performed by the administration. I thought I was the first psychologist hired by the Program. In fact, I was the second. There was a woman working in child psychiatry who was paid by the Program but never gave any service within the Program. Fortunately we learned of this embarrassment before the first major site visit. We gave the administration "hell" but put on a good face.

It was not uncommon for the administration to fail to notify NIMH of staff assignment changes which might have been in the interest of giving service where it was needed. Come the day of a site visit, the staff member in question might drop his jaw and sit wide-eyed as he learned what the site visitors thought his job was. He would have to scramble to cover up the fact that he knew nothing about his "real" job description.

Another service area of the Program that was not properly developed was the virtually nonexistent day care program. Although the grant called for a small, again largely inadequate staff, it existed as an ancillary service run by the inpatient staff. Because there was primary emphasis on preventive consultation and education and outpatient programs, these day care personnel tended to be viewed unfairly as non-essential. If there had been a better liaison with the state mental hospitals and a touch of creativity, there might have been a chronic-patient-oriented day care program. Of course, there was the genuine fear that the day care program might simply become an outpatient arm for chronically ill state hospital patients.

Most of the staff at the outpatient satellites had a problem with the concept of who belonged as a day care patient. In our view, the entire inner city population could have used a "break" by going into the day care program, at least from time to time. We never seemed able to sort out what the program was about and how it fit in the spectrum of services. In that regard we all failed.

Another major problem we had to deal with was what we called "dumping". The staff wanted to give service and most city programs were more than happy to try to dump their most troublesome and chronic cases on our doorstep. It wasn't that we weren't interested in dealing with difficult cases. However, we had quickly learned that there were people who chronically floated from agency to agency without ever being able to connect with helpful services. To blindly accept "dumping" would have bled the staff of time and taken services away from people who would benefit. Choices had to be made and we became quite clear that we had to know when to "quit".

In short, a talented and willing staff was saddled with control by the two competing institutionalized structures of the State and the University, and some inappropriate behavior on the part of the staff could be traced by and large to weak and uneven administration. The problem was made more serious by the interference of some mental health officials who behaved in such a manner as to divert time and energy away from services to defense of the Program. More about the interference later.

But possibly the greatest tragedy was the failure to monitor and evaluate a groundbreaking type of program. The Program was supposed to be a laboratory for the development of techniques for delivering service and training. It should have been evaluated and close contact maintained by the State in order to gain knowledge from the experiences, successes, and mistakes of the staff. No such thing ever happened, and for a long time our statistics were never even entered in state statistics. State officials knew little or nothing about the Program and the supposed plan for using it as a training ground to seed other developing programs in the state never was actualized. Accommodations for training purposes could have been made, but the staff was very assertive and was not going to be bulldozed. It would have to have been a partnership.

A program strong in service with flexibility and a staff that learned quickly had come into being. There was a great deal learned and advances made in the delivery of effective services. In later chapters the lessons learned will be addressed.

THE AUTHOR'S ROLE

Except for my time as an intern at Duke University Medical Center I had not worked for a long period of time delivering service in an institutional setting. My main assets were youthful enthusiasm, solid clinical training, idealism, and the expectation that the promise of the movement could be realized (naivete). I was also well-versed in the theoretical underpinnings of community mental health.

Youthful enthusiasm turned out to be my saving grace. It soon became obvious that it was totally naive to assume that young professionals could conceivably know how to deliver service to an impoverished population with whom we shared very little in the way of cultural background. The theory of community mental health was hard to apply to the day-to-day realities of the population we were to serve. And the theory was equally hard to apply to the delivery of consultation and education services, at least in the initial stages. Somehow it was assumed that we would be arriving from the Olympus of academia and deliver the mental health scriptures.

I was assigned to the first outpatient unit to open. We were given offices directly above the delivery entrance for hospital supplies. My job was to give psychotherapy to clients who had not yet arrived because no one knew of our existence. It was our job to make the population and agencies aware of our existence and the "marvelous" expertise we had to offer. Our first satellite director was a very nice psychiatrist who knew little more than we did, and so we floundered together. Our secretary at first had nothing to do but gradually became overwhelmed. And supplies failed to arrive, so there were times when we had to go out and purchase supplies ourselves. To overcome this funding problem we installed a Coke machine, which I was enthusiastic about because I drank a lot of soda. Having the supply staff of the hospital downstairs proved a boon because they purchased sodas from our machine and the proceeds were used to buy office supplies.

Young clinicians had to learn how to administer as well, and we were ever so well-intentioned. One of our secretaries had a husband who was a heroin addict. Virtually every morning she came to work in tears. We were solicitous and inadvertently supported her misery. She finally left to take a job at General Motors, where they were not solicitous; she discovered a refuge away from family problems and found her way to a stable life.

Being a small staff we had to step into various roles. After I became director of the unit, there was one day when neither of the secretaries showed up. I stepped in to answer the phones. I had had no idea what kind of abuse the secretaries took.

There were traditional expectations, and in addition to giving therapy I was also expected to do psychological testing. At least for that I was reasonably prepared.

As an intern I had been given the poor of Durham to test, and so I was prepared for what worked and what did not work and what to expect. What was to be done with the results was another matter entirely. Sometimes it was helpful diagnostically with adults if they could figure how to respond to such things as the Thematic Apperception Test or the Rorschach Inkblot Test. So, I had to develop my own norms. As to the children, the validity of the intelligence tests was highly questionable, and I soon found that the median IQ was 85. Not only were the children disadvantaged but the material was foreign to them.

And then there was the consultation and education activities we were to provide. Fortunately, the first thing we had to do was to make agencies in the area aware of our existence so they would refer people to us. So, our first visit was a matter of getting acquainted, which gave us structure so we did not make complete fools of ourselves by making pompous statements and offering excessive promises. More about the issue of consultation later.

Our staff swiftly became a fine working unit. We were not only dedicated and, because we had little interference from above (they didn't care), we could learn what we should do and should not do.

Within two years the program was beginning to learn that the type of work we were doing did not require a psychiatrist as a unit director. And so I was invited to meet with the Head of the Psychiatric Institute. The meeting began with him loftily declaring that I seemed uncomfortable. On that point he was right; I was aware that our work was not valued and I did not trust him at all. It was meant, of course, to put me off guard and in my place. I learned they wanted me to become the first nonpsychiatrist to head a mental health unit in the State of Maryland. It was not flattering. It was a discount. But the job was mine. For the first time I became a chief among my Indian peers.

Now that I was important, I was invited to meet with the other psychologists at the Institute. I was given papers to review for a professional journal, a task that interested me not at all. It seemed to me that they were all reasonably competently done. The first formal meeting was about how to make psychologists look good to the psychiatric staff. I never went back.

My staff, as they now were, did not need much in the way of supervision since they were all more than competent, knew their jobs and their limits. We needed to consult with each other and solve problems together. We agreed to have two formal meetings per week. One was administrative to ensure a smoothly running unit and one for sharing our concerns about clinical issues. Our doors were always open to each other and we consulted freely.

Administratively I had to attend meetings in the central office. They were a trying experience, dealing with matters which concerned our staff not at all, but they did help me head off policies that would disrupt my staff and their ability to deliver service.

At a unit administrative meeting one day I was dutifully reporting on events at the central office. The staff was unusually restless. I asked, "Do you want to hear about this?" There came a loud chorus of "no" and they indicated they trusted me to manage it and that they simply found what was happening centrally not only distressing but unnecessary for them to know. So I assumed the virtual "position" with my arms over my head, fingers locked as I shed disruptive interference from the central office. It was my job to protect my staff so they could do their jobs. We

10

subsequently confined our work in the administrative meeting to the needs of our unit. They trusted me to defend their interests and the interests of our clients.

And so I became Dr. No. No, my staff did not need the kind of training proposed. No, we would not accept medical students coming for a six-week rotation to see our clients. It required diplomacy, but when something was declined, it was done quietly and firmly and ended with a strongly implied period. It was not as difficult as it might seem since the central administration had become accustomed to a very independent staff and they were generally passive in contrast to the activism of the line staff. The different orientations between the staff, the administration, the University, and the State had created a chasm which could not be bridged.

Our unit was efficiently delivering services to a population of 40,000 people and engaging in the form of consultation we had found effective. We needed to be left alone.

ISSUES IN THE SOCIAL CONTEXT

We have seen how the Program began, but the essence of its development was found in the nature of the community served. The area served by the Program included some of the most depressed and depressing poverty-stricken sections of Baltimore, as well as many stable working-class neighborhoods and to a more limited extent, small ethnic communities that lent a certain heterogeneity and, at times, charm to the scene. There were some well-maintained neighborhoods with scrubbed marble stairs and ornate doors as well as blocks and blocks of decaying inner city rowhouses.

A precise demographic portrait of the catchment area is not necessary here. Suffice it to say that this section of the city had one of the highest admission rates to state hospitals, and for other variables such as delinquency, crime, illegitimacy, drug abuse, poverty, alcoholism, etc. it was almost invariably on the worst end of any statistical distribution.

In some regards the population of the catchment area was homogenous especially when it came to socioeconomic status and the experience of a high-stress environment. With minor exceptions the population was lower middle-class and below. The area was reasonably split between Black and White populations.

As to terminology, African-Americans will be referred to as Black. In the preceding years descriptive terms had moved from Negro to Colored and finally to Black which was at last declared to be "beautiful". That stuck with me and my peers. The later use of African-American often seemed clinical to me.

Whatever Happened to Community Mental Health?

The Black area was a center of considerable Poverty Program activity and neighborhood groups designed for various activist purposes and, in general, it was a fertile area for the development of socially oriented problem solving.

The White community, in contrast, was much more traditional in its viewpoints, was less inclined to participate in Poverty Program activities, and was a mixed population of long-term residents, ethnic minorities, and immigrants from Appalachia.

The issues in this population were not easily reduced to racial discrimination, crime, drugs, a declining economic environment, and environmental deterioration. Moreover, it is not appropriate to view the inner city population as merely a sea of impoverished Black people fighting for survival in a racist society. To fully catalogue the ills and root causes of inner city misery is difficult and not useful in this work. But there are a few points illustrating important issues.

If there was a root cause of the problems in the catchment area it might be summed up as a function of social class with generous overlays of other diverse problems. The people we were working with were the "left behinds". Few Black people were making it into the middle class at the time, but the population we dealt with, as a whole, had come from disadvantaged positions and had not found hoped-for opportunities.

Many of the Black people had emigrated from the rural South seeking work further north. They came with few skills to cope with a complex urban environment. Race simply made their lives more difficult. And then with educational deficiencies, nutritional deficiencies, and poor health care their plight was intensified.

Many of the White community came from insular and proud Appalachian communities and similarly came with few skills to cope with the urban environment. As the economic well-being of the mountain areas continued to decline, many of them sought advantages assumed to exist in Baltimore.

When it came to giving them mental health services, professionals all too often brought traditional psychotherapeutic models and techniques not applicable to this population. And, for the White population, their needs were often overlooked because of an inappropriate racial focus.

The word *ghetto* became widely used during the civil rights era. It generally referred to the confinement of a Black population by virtue of overt and covert discrimination. Yet, the White population was often every bit as ghettoized. These people included lower class Whites, blue-collar workers confined by employment and family ties.

Appalachian Whites who migrated to Baltimore during and after World War II represented a distinct subgroup, as did ethnic groups; though well established, they were often confined by familial and cultural ties as well. Both of these groups faced particular problems but in many ways were strikingly similar in that they were often overwhelmed by the stresses of their lives and our staff had to respond accordingly.

Early on, the staff had to adjust their perspective. Without guidance from more senior staff it was up to us to shape our own views. In this regard a young Black woman social worker was crucial in helping me gain perspective. Roz Griffin was my right arm and my mentor. She came with experience in Baltimore's inner city and a sharp, discerning mind.

By rights she should have been chosen as the unit director but sexism, racism, and the professional hierarchy bias determined the choice. In fact, she said that she never knew why she was promoted. She was, being a woman and Black, what we called a "twofer".

We were on our own in determining our approach, and her perspective was crucial. As we made a place for ourselves in the area of services increasing numbers of people came through the clinic doors. There were many people who were suffering from chronic psychotic illnesses and relatively few who could be classified as suffering from classical neuroses. Aside from issues of drugs and alcohol, which generally required referral to other community resources, it was necessary to look at the true nature and origin of the problems the majority of the population faced.

Most of our patients clearly demonstrated symptoms of anxiety and depression. It became a dark joke among the staff that, given their lives, there had to be something wrong with them if they were not either anxious, depressed or both. And so we established a position of "assumed normalcy". Their reactions and feelings were born of a chaotic environment in which day-to-day life was a challenge of survival.

Women often expressed a deep-rooted mistrust of men and, indeed, there was a shortage of stable men on whom they could rely and find a warm partnership which fed them emotionally. The most common initial sexual experience was rape.

Men fared little better. Their job skills were limited and genuine opportunities few and far between. Jobs often had to be sought in far away areas of the city or even in the suburbs, which meant punishing commutes using uneven and limited public transportation. If they maintained a family life, it was filled with children challenged by school problems and health problems among many other things. The women were exhausted, and satisfying time together was limited.

This was our context and the view we had to establish in order to respond to the people who came through our doors for service. Later I will discuss the specific model which was developed.

FINDING THE COMMUNITY

The word "community" presented a problem to the staff. Constantly we had to wrestle with the meaning of the word. We came to know we were dealing with a series of communities and that our work had to focus on their needs and how to help them.

There was something missing in the whole idea of "community" mental health. In order to get outpatient services moving it was essential to go out and make contact -with what? On this we received little guidance except from Carl, our head community organizer. In order to respond, the staff as a whole had to become community organizers.

We were charged to deliver consultation and education services, but in this chaotic environment the open question was to whom and about what. And so the approach was broken down into distinct layers. Community agencies were approached in order to build relationships and get referrals. That meant defining ourselves and what we could and could not do. It became bewildering. We needed liaison with drug and alcohol treatment programs to refer out and could offer them separate services not specifically related to substance abuse. Relating to the Community Action Agency, where poverty program activities were central, was essential.

Very little at the beginning related to giving consultation and education. We had relationships to establish and we had to learn what we were doing. Certainly we had little to offer in many ways. The tablets with wisdom given from above were blank.

The staff was constantly at odds about how to define leaders of the community. There were so many and so many claims. There was no cohesive entity or structure, and it was impossible to locate reliable spokesmen and leaders. Each person had to be assessed, each claim validated and we had to forever be aware of hidden agendas. Often they were not reaching out for resources but for some personal benefit, which might be tangible or simply be ego enhancement and recognition. Staff meetings and consultations often revolved around discussions about outreach to organizations without touching on clinical issues with given clients.

And then there were barriers. In planning the program, lines for service were drawn on a map. In the abstract no one could know what was being included or what inclusion implied.

14

The first clinic was at the edge of the university campus; shortly we had to move farther out into the catchment area. The choice of location was not an easy one. Ultimately a location very near the racial dividing line of Baltimore Street was chosen. Our expectation that both Black and White would come to the location proved to be correct. It was also well served by bus service. It would have been all too easy to confine service to one group of residents simply by virtue of choice of location.

SUMMARY

Community mental health in that era was best characterized in its theory as having the best of intentions. Then reality reared its ugly head. In this situation, services had to be delivered and a viable program developed by a young, inexperienced staff beset by the competing interests of the State and the University.

A willing staff was thrown onto the streets to develop clinical services and be community organizers. The community sought did not exist and the true form of the program had to be developed from the ground up.

But a reform movement was under way, and there was optimism and a belief that success could be found. Such movements attract particular kinds of tenacious and dedicated people. And so we clung together, determined to build a system which would serve a seriously disadvantaged population.

Chapter 2
Therapeutic and Service Issues with the Poor

CONTEXT

For most mental health professionals trained in the 1960s, basic studies of psychotherapy began with the work of Freud which, as we know, had origins in the treatment of middle-class and upper-middle-class Viennese. Insight and fundamental change were the goals as an "onion" was peeled. Later, In many training settings, the patient population might be limited to middle-class patients. Treating the poor was often a relatively rare experience. For a variety of reasons the poor did not receive services which were effective for them, and it was often thought that their problems were a matter of motivation and personal shortcomings. Less traditional and alternative methods of intervention were generally not considered. Only later did the professions come to accept the possibility that the sociocultural environment or life circumstances might be major contributors to "maladaptive functioning".

In this chapter the emphasis is on services provided in an outpatient satellite center in an inner city setting with the goal of effective intervention. Our focus will be on what was learned that enabled the staff to be effective. But first, it is necessary to look at the life experience of the clients and how it might have conditioned their responses to what was offered in the way of help.

THE MENTAL HEALTH HERITAGE OF THE POOR

In approaching the task of delivering services the staff learned quickly that it was essential to pay attention both to the prior experience of area residents when they sought service and what "mental health" and "mental illness" meant to them.

Whatever Happened to Community Mental Health?

We learned that mental illness meant either that the person was "crazy" or that there might well be police intervention. In their neighborhoods they observed deeply disturbed people roaming the streets who were not integral to the community. A disturbance involving a mentally ill person might begin simply enough but, when there was no effective help, it might quickly progress to a more disturbing level. Rarely could the suffering be purely private and the individuals were irritants to the community. Such people were feared and shunned. Psychotic individuals were much more visible than people who suffered quietly from depression or anxiety. Mental illness intruded in numerous and disturbing ways.

At times a neighbor or family member might feel it necessary to intervene on behalf of a person who was clearly in difficulty. Intervention often meant seeking treatment in the person's "best interest" . There were few options, and intervention usually meant calling the police. Psychotic individuals could be forcibly removed from their homes or the street if they were viewed as being a public nuisance or were seen as likely to hurt themselves or others.

If a relative was involved, then the relative would go before a municipal court judge and testify to the fact that the person was a danger to himself or others. A warrant on a technical charge of disturbing the peace was issued, and the individual was taken into custody by the police, often in a spectacular event. He or she would be taken to a lockup to await examination by two physicians, who invariably certified them as requiring treatment for their own benefit. They might wait as long as twenty-four hours without medication or sympathetic contact and, if violent, might be denied the use of toilet facilities and meals. Eventually they were transferred to a state mental hospital, possibly in handcuffs.

The most likely treatment was medication and, other than in an intake interview, they were unlikely to receive much in the way of personal therapeutic intervention. The film *One Flew Over the Cuckoos Nest* presents a picture of mental health care that was often all too accurate. The patients learned the value of being cooperative and quiet and that this would lead to an early discharge.

They were generally discharged highly medicated and referred to a clinic to which they typically did not go. The cycle repeated itself and they seemed to be "social waste" that required recycling.

The police were forced to use the methods and resources at their disposal and found the task thoroughly distasteful. Over time the judges became less inclined to be involved. As years passed and the tide turned against funding public hospitals, the mentally ill were left to wander the streets. With the decline of the reform movement and funds being cut for affordable housing, the mentally ill were joined in the streets by families, often headed by a single mother. The end result was the presence of homeless individuals and families we see wandering the streets today.

In cases of less severe pathology, the person might go to a public clinic. In the inner city this typically meant treatment by often disinterested psychiatric residents or medical students on a six-week rotation. They typically had little interest in treating people who could not benefit from "insight therapy".

In such clinics the patient underwent a mental status examination that they found thoroughly mystifying. It did not touch on the real problems in their lives. The Program staff heard negative statements regarding what the patients considered "foolish questions" usually asked in an aloof fashion without explanation. Medication was commonly prescribed and, if the person returned, he might see a string of medical students on short-term rotations. In some fashion he was "training" the medical students but was not being treated in an effective fashion.

The staff was warned time and time again by University personnel that our client population would not be timely and would frequently miss appointments. We were told to expect that most of the clients would not return for a second appointment and that they could not benefit from intervention.

What we quickly learned was that first sessions in most clinic settings were characterized by the following:

- The interview was done by a disinterested professional whose negative expectations had already been set.
- An implicit assumption was that only candidates for insight therapy were desired.
- Medication was usually the only real help offered.
- An "alien", unexplained mental status examination was given.
- No assistance with reality problems was offered.
- "Professional" distance was imposed.

This history meant that one of the first jobs of the staff was to educate members of the community to the purposes of the clinic and making it clear that sympathetic help was available and that it could include advocacy on their behalf. The educational problem extended to personnel of other agencies who had to properly prepare the people to utilize the services. Only gradually was it possible to overcome a long history of mismanagement that initially led the poor to believe the mental health worker was to be feared.

MEDICAL MODEL LIMITATIONS

The staff initially struggled with the applicability of the medical model and the terms *patient* and *client*. "Client" was generally preferred, although it was impossible not to use "patient" at times and often they were used interchangeably. It was not long before it was clear to the staff that the medical model was not a good fit.

Long ago efforts were made to have mental illness taken under the wing of medicine so that the problems could be removed from theology. But our emotional and cognitive lives and related dysfunctions were difficult to describe as a disease. A diagnosis was meant to indicate a form of treatment which, in regard to mental illness, was often quite unclear. Description of suffering is one thing, the needed form of intervention quite another.

The population of the inner city of Baltimore was burdened by a difficult environment, and in many instances the culture they brought from the South and Appalachia did not serve them well.

The realistic plight of women in the inner city was particularly instructive. In those days women's liberation was just beginning and had not filtered down to the poor. Stable men were hard to find, whether they were Black or White. The economic and social system operated to make "normal" family life difficult at best.

All too often the woman who struggled alone with her children or tried to have a satisfactory heterosexual relationship were victimized by the views of professionals. Rather than viewing her as needing help, support, and guidance in a difficult environment, she was often assessed as being a person who perpetuated her difficulties. She might well feel stigmatized.

The staff found it essential to have a perspective which involved understanding the impact of social class, cultural heritage, the social structure of the environment, and how "family" functioned in the inner city, in addition to the stresses of poverty. A woman's response to short-term and long-term problems needed to be optimized with attendant reduction of stress and distress. Rigid adherence to the medical model simply did not work. The "prescription" for action was found in a response to the reality of her existence and how she needed to respond to it with an ally by her side.

DIAGNOSIS AND TREATMENT

Issues of diagnosis and treatment relate closely to the use of the medical model, and it may be necessary to label a person. Labeling assists the clinician in organizing his thinking and may provide a framework for a person reading a record in the future. Unfortunately, however, labeling may not reveal much about basic causative factors and the most desirable form of intervention.

For example, inner city parents face a problem common to all parents. During early childhood the child is under clear parental control, but then comes the inevitability of adolescence with increasing independence and the need to let the child loosen ties and move out into the larger world. It was common to have adolescents brought in with complaints about misbehavior at school, "hooking" school, disobeying parental orders, court involvement after an incident of theft, or "going with the wrong crowd".

A typical diagnosis would be "adjustment reaction of adolescence". However, the issues often went well beyond essentially "normal" issues for the age group. There might not be a viable parental partnership, and such children routinely lived in a particularly dangerous environment. Worse, the parent was not just concerned but often was experiencing panic. With panic they were totally unable to exercise sound parental authority. The dangers were real where there were drugs, a high level of crime, and a very difficult peer environment.

Focusing on the adjustment issues of the child alone ignored a focus on the family unit, the well-being of other children in the family, and the tenuous existence of a person who might well be a single parent. A strong alliance between the clinician and the parent was indicated, and the clinician might well have to become a form of a parent as well as working to mobilize community resources. Decreasing the panic of a parent in such an environment was essential, as was assessment of the other children in the household. If problems including such things as untreated physical health problems were stressing the family unit, they contributed to increasing the parental panic. In the inner city, the family, not the identified child, was the "patient". Resources and attention to the stress on the mother might be just as essential if not more essential. Thus, we sought continually to catalogue stresses and find resources.

Another example relates to a woman who came to the clinic complaining of "bad nerves". Common diagnoses would have been "anxiety reaction" or "depressive reaction" if nothing more fundamental was found. The staff felt it was important to distinguish between anxiety and fear. There was a lot to be feared in the inner city, and concern about the dangers did not reflect imaginary or irrational perceptions of dangers.

In one case a referral came from the local Community Action Agency (CAA), the arm of the Poverty Program. Under such circumstances a CAA staffer would often accompany the clinician on a home visit. Being accompanied fostered the development of the relationship between the potential client and the clinician.

On such visits it was essential to be prepared for anything. The first indicator was typically the door of the rowhouse. The exterior walls were usually brick or Formstone which was an artificial material that looked like stone. But the condition of the door told everything. In this case, the door looked like it had been through an attack of some sort. The stairway was grim and the apartment indicated extreme poverty. It was essential to be gracious and sit on furniture that was decrepit and might be crawling with insects.

After the introduction, the woman poured out her story. She did not seem to be exhibiting marked behavioral or emotional abnormalities. Her life was a war story of survival. Her two daughters were struggling in school and her son was retarded. She was a single mother, on welfare, lacking in self-confidence who felt depressed and nervous. For her there seemed to be no future to look forward to.

Her history indicated an exceedingly difficult childhood not unlike what her own children were experiencing. It seemed her current emotional circumstances could be traced in part to her background of experiences. One view would have been that psychotherapy regarding her past might open ways to improve her functioning and feelings of well-being.

She was meek, tearful and nervous but held her ground against the idea of exploring past pain and suffering. At that moment she held the key to her own 'therapy". We were forced to organize the problems around her being on welfare, "getting nowhere", the poverty of gratification, and the problems facing her children.

And so we turned to the reality of her circumstances. She clearly needed a high school diploma and a referral to the Division of Vocational Rehabilitation was arranged. In those days we were free to establish a disability so education and training could be paid for. The woman from the CAA knew of grandmothers in the area who would take the children in the short term if their mother returned late from her educational program. We designed a community-based support network and I formed a supportive relationship with her. A relationship was also formed with her children.

In the end she received her high school equivalency certificate and she gained a good training position in one of the health systems. Her self-confidence soared, her depression and nervousness subsided, and when the family became self sufficient they moved to a more pleasant environment.

In short, her situation had been genuinely depressing, and she had realistic fears for herself and her children. To have sought amelioration in psychotherapy aimed at removing so-called psychopathology might actually have made matters worse and would not have helped her build a future for herself and her children. Her symptoms were reality-based.

It sounds so simple in the telling but the reality was that in many clinic settings the real issues on which the symptoms were based were easily overlooked, possibly because the resources for alternative interventions might not be available.

In fact, the necessary resources were at hand and did not involve extensive effort. Of course not everyone is easily mobilized but this story was common in our experience.

Naturally we had to engage in triage. There were people who could not be helped and we had to know when to "quit". And, there were people who benefited from therapy as well as chronic cases of psychosis who required ongoing attention. But, the major part of our work related to helping with the reality of their environment, and it resulted in substantial "mental health" benefits.

SERVICE DELIVERY IN THE WESTERN SATELLITE CENTER

The five core services of outpatient, inpatient, consultation and education, emergency, and day care were to be delivered to the people of the catchment area. On a day-to-day basis, particularly at the beginning, the primary focus of activity was in the outpatient service centers. Consultation and education (C & E) had to be begun first, because we had to acquaint the agencies and the public with our existence and what we could and could not do. In unintended ways C & E shaped the development of the program. And rather than delivering wisdom from the heights of academia, we received revelations from the streets, the rowhouses and the projects. The public and the realities of their lives shaped the views and activities of the newly arrived professionals.

As mentioned, the very first satellite center was located in available space at the edge of the University campus. Shortly we moved out to the very center of the action and became the Western Satellite Center. It served a racially mixed population which was fairly homogenous in social class. The staff was clear about the racial balance, but visitors from the State, University and Federal government had to be constantly reminded that we were not "the Black center". Where confusion existed within the staff at large, it reflected the romanticism attached to working in the inner city. For most of the staff working away from the University, romanticism was short-lived. Our training and our illusions were under assault as we worked with more interference than support from our supervising institutions.

As to the White community, it was frequently misperceived by others as uniformly prejudiced, conservative, and generally less interested in services because their attitudes were not in harmony with the tenor of the reform movement. While some of these assumptions had some truth to them, it did not change the fact that the White community was every bit as under attack as was the Black community. State officials had their misperceptions reinforced by the presence of better-organized Black activist groups. They seemed to form a community with whom the state officials could relate. Working with the White community proved more time-consuming.

In its original location it was clear that the outpatient facility was inhibited in its functioning by being relatively hidden from view, in close proximity to the University, and by space limitations. It was considered inadequate by the staff, state officials, and site visitors from the NIMH. A protracted space search was undertaken. Interestingly enough, however, even though state officials decried the inadequacy of the original facility, there was no real assurance that the State would pay the rent on another facility. Only when the University indicated a strong desire for the return of its building, which it had provided free of charge, was there serous support for finding another facility.

There were a number of requirements to be met in finding a more suitable facility. First, priority was attached to finding something that genuinely fronted on a community so that entry was unimpeded and relatedness to the area would be maximized. Second, it needed to be reasonably central to the area served so that many people would be able to walk to the center if at all possible. Third, for those forced to take the bus, it needed to be accessible to major routes running in all directions. Fourth, it seemed crucial for it to be on or near the street forming the racial dividing line.

The search for space was an eye-opening experience in itself. Some of the most dilapidated structures imaginable were toured. The most common question was, "When does the bulldozer arrive?" It was clear that, despite the large number of vacant buildings, few were suitable for renovation or habitation. Such might also have been said of many buildings with numerous tenants.

Finally the staff member serving as the lead scout found a jewel of a 16- room, three-story rowhouse which would serve well with a modicum of renovation. It should be mentioned that rents were generally exorbitant in such an area and it might have been easier to find a moderately priced dwelling in a suburb. The staff was delighted to find that the landlord was a charming old gentleman who proposed a reasonable rent when compared with what had been quoted elsewhere. He would take care of renovations and prorate the additional cost over five years.

The staff was gratified to find someone who was not indigenous to the community, had worked for years building a real estate business, and actually wanted to give something back to the community. We were considerably less gratified by the despicable treatment he received from the State in the negotiations and in the work to renovate the building. In the end we were grateful for his having produced a more than serviceable building.

The building was located one half-block off the commercial street which served the White and Black communities and was considered neutral territory. It fronted directly on a major cross street where there were nearby bus stops for routes leading in all directions. A survey of the area residents revealed no objections to the presence of the clinic, and their general neutrality continued after the move.

When the facility was finally renovated and the clinic doors were opened, the clients and visitors from other organizations expressed approval. It was clear they liked what had been done with an existing structure in character with the neighborhood. The choice of location was further vindicated in that there was no trouble enticing current clients to come and new clients continued to reflect the 50-50 racial balance of the area as a whole.

With the opening of the Western Satellite Center consolidation of services could take place and the approach to delivering services was finalized. By this time the staff was clear about their service model, which involved:

- Open walk-in clinics each morning and one evening a week. No appointments were necessary. The secretarial staff helped the client fill out the initial paperwork.
- All people who came were seen that morning, although other available staff might have to be called in for intake service in case there was an unusually large number of people.
- Intake interviews did not have a rigid time format. Depending upon the problem the intake might be brief or prolonged.
- In most instances anyone seen that morning became the client of the clinician who interviewed him or her.

- Unless there was a clear reason to assume otherwise, the client was considered to be "normal" and, while the interview was open to what was needed, the main focus would be on understanding their lives and the stresses from which they suffered. Anxiety and depression were assumed to reflect their environmental experience and life situation.
- The initial assumption of normalcy in a difficult environment always stood to be proved wrong. If intervention proved to be ineffective at this level, then the approach was altered and the approach reassessed. This process meant an economy of effort.
- Following the morning walk-in clinic the clinician would spend the afternoon organizing interventions reflective of the problems faced by the new client. Medical records or consultations were sought, calls were made to related agencies such as the office in a project, resources were sought through the Community Action Agency etc. In short a beginning was made to solve problems and relieve stress as quickly as possible.
- Another appointment was given as soon as required whether the next day or the following week.

In a sense we had a prime directive: "Go into the client's world, learn about it and then help them with it." One way to look at it was that we were "life management coaches".

The entire initial intake was framed around the view of the client coming from a stressful, high-problem life circumstance. Commonly this form of intervention yielded swift short-term gains and enduring gains.

Once the initial problems were evaluated and moves made to ameliorate them, there could be another assessment. In a minority of cases there were people who benefited from traditional psychotherapy. In others, it was apparent that there was a severe, chronic condition which required a very different kind of intervention.

For purposes of the walk-in clinic, staff members were not differentiated as to professional discipline. Our basic approach could be handled by any professional discipline, and specifics would come into play later as necessary. On any given morning the new client might be seen by a social worker, psychologist, psychiatric nurse or (later) one of our most promising mental health associates or community workers. Early on, a full-time psychiatrist shared equal walk-in responsibilities.

There was never any such thing as a waiting list. Even under pressing circumstances the staff was flexible and would pitch in as needed. Such a response was crucial because the clients were typically crisis oriented. They came for help only when it was essential.

In the case of children brought to the clinic, the clinician serving walk-in clinic did not necessarily retain the case because it was inappropriate to assume that every staff member had the requisite skills or the interest. Accordingly, the staff member prepared a report, gathered information from outside agencies and presented the material on the case to a biweekly conference with a child psychiatrist and child psychologist. In the conference it would be decided whether continuing therapy was needed, what medical evaluations were desirable, if there was a need for a psychological evaluation, and which staff member with expertise in treating children would take the case. Thus, each staff member served a generic function but specific expertise would be called upon as needed. Even though a child might be presented as the problem, the family was never forgotten.

At times the child was a front for presenting a parent's problem; the original clinician would most often continue with the family or mother. This arrangement was the most economical one possible in that with an uncertain walk-in clinical load, it was impossible to afford the luxury of having two clinicians on duty, one with child therapy expertise and one with adult expertise, waiting for people who came without an appointment. It represented the minimum possible in a wait-for service. Until the case was presented in child conference, information from other institutions was being gathered.

Not every case involving adolescents and adults was discussed in a staff conference. Any new staff person given walk-in clinic responsibility was assumed to be able to manage the cases under reasonable supervision. No new staff member ever fought this policy. Almost no one ever came who was experienced in this kind of setting using this kind of approach. The first morning on walk-in clinic alone was a terrifying experience. That we were able to function this way was also indicative of our fortunate position in being able to hire the people whom we hired.

Economy of staff time was essential. New patients did not have to see numerous people for evaluations unless absolutely necessary and the staff did not have to spend long hours in mandatory conferences. Everyone was encouraged to bring problem cases or incidents of interest to the weekly staff clinical conference. Our doors were always open and collateral opinions always available.

Given the immediacy of the client population's problems, discussion of cases often took place informally and at the needed time when the crisis was being met. the formal and informal consultation worked well in the setting. The check on a staff member who might be performing poorly was simple enough. The staff was small, and it was impossible to hide mismanagement of cases for long. The greatest danger over time was "burnout". The effective life of a clinician in such a setting usually did not extend beyond five years. It was the job of staff, but especially the director, to be alert to the signs of staff burnout.

It was unnecessary, if not impossible, to obtain a routine psychiatric or psychological evaluation on every new case. Evaluations were sought from the consulting psychiatrists when differential questions were at issue and when there was, in the eyes of the clinician (not necessarily the client) a need for medication. Newer staff members tended to consult the psychiatrists more often than the experienced staff consulted the psychiatrists.

In regard to psychological evaluations, for which I was generally responsible, I tended to discourage them for reasons in addition to time limitations. I viewed most requests for psychological evaluations as being "hunting operations" and was wholly sympathetic only in cases where there was a differential question involved - such as a question of borderline psychosis or brain damage. In practice the staff tended to get along quite well without routine psychological evaluations. In cases where an inappropriate request was forwarded to me, I either helped the clinician clarify the issues or referred them to their supervisor to decide on the merits of the request or to formulate a more concise and pointed request.

There were specific procedures for integrating new staff coming to the center. No one, regardless of his or her background or training was given immediate clinical assignment. Each new person would sit in with a clinician experienced for the setting until he or she developed a concept of the needs of the clients and began to have some working knowledge of the agencies that would be involved in the assignment.

It was not a matter of knowing the agencies, it was a matter of knowing the reality of the agencies. Directories of services were available and, on paper at least, it looked as though every conceivable service was available and working effectively. Reality was quite another matter. There were gargantuan holes in services available, and there was a marked difference in how well agencies functioned.

Huge amounts of time could be wasted (staff's and client's) looking for resources that did not exist. We also could not make the assumption that a clinician, no matter how experienced, would know how to work with our client population. Clinicians new to this type of program often came experienced with middle-class individuals and were not used to dealing with the severity of reality problems found in the inner city. In addition, if one had never dealt with poverty related programs, welfare systems, housing project management, etc., it was necessary to gain some understanding of the politics, rules and orientations of these agencies. It was also helpful to know exactly who to call. And when regular, structured supervision was clearly no longer necessary, they still had easy access to more experienced persons and their contacts in other agencies.

And then there was the matter of personal safety. The staff was not "house bound". They not only had to confront difficult situations while in the office but they had to walk the gritty streets and climb the urine-soaked stairs of the projects. They had to know when to back out of a rowhouse and determine when their own safety might be at risk. In short, they had to develop "street smarts" which did not happen overnight. They were encouraged to seek consultation regarding when or when not to make a home visit and to ask for escort when necessary.

It should be emphasized that the experience in the Program happened a long time ago when, believe it or not, the inner city was a safer place. It was during a reform movement and efforts were being made to make contact and to make changes. In some ways the worker in the inner city environment had a contract with the residents, a contract which, in some areas, probably no longer exists. Nonetheless, it was a dangerous environment. And what was remarkable was that we kept ourselves and each other safe. We had no major incidents.

On the issue of supervision, supervisors were not assigned according to discipline but according to availability, skill, and that ephemeral quality of "good fit". Some newcomers were inclined to be aggressive and had to be toned down. Others were anxious and needed support. A person of another discipline might be the perfect supervisor based on temperament and experience rather than fund of knowledge or procedures. It worked because the required skills were assembled. The staff developed clinical skills, diplomacy, knowledge of resources, warmth, and a willingness to meet the client where he was and to work on solving the problems stressing him or her. The presence of all major disciplines existing on an equal footing was useful in that the staff could learn from each other's approaches and fund of knowledge. Thus, in conference, all of the staff had something to learn and could broaden their own capacity to respond. For informal consultation, a variety of necessary expertise was available to perform the job. This flexible melding of different disciplines was growth inducing and added immeasurable flexibility to the organization.

Obviously, the staff did not function as a team in treating clients; each professional discipline "did their thing" with each client. Rather, functioning as a team was informal and the differential skills of the staff were brought together as they learned and grew through mutual, shared experiences. Staff persons were hired because they were competent to do the job, and individuals were sought with enough skill and responsibility to take primary treatment duties. Teams comprising representatives of each of the major disciplines were in vogue in some settings at the time, but for us to have a representative of each profession interview each client would have been a waste of staff time and the client's time when he or she was in distress.

So, each staff member took their turn with occasional referral to another staff member with special expertise. Continuity of care with the original clinician was assumed. If hospitalization was required, that person maintained contact. A high level of contact was rarely possible on the Program's inpatient unit because the service offered such a concentrated program that the outpatient clinician often felt inessential except as a reassuring link with the outside world. It was generally difficult to continue therapy as before because the short term hospitalization often left the person "talked out" at least temporarily. When the client was released from the hospital, regular sessions resumed.

Because so many clients were crisis oriented, there were numerous instances of people coming in during a period of crisis and then being terminated until they felt that they needed to return. When they returned, it was assumed, unless there was a good reason not to, that they would return to the same therapist. Life was such an ongoing struggle in the inner city environment that it would have been naive to assume client's lives could be put in order and they would live happily ever after.

Continuity of care included other elements. Clinicians had to be prepared to intervene with numerous outside agencies when asked by the client. Such requests might come after "termination" and constituted continuing assistance in "life maintenance". It was assumed that the clinician would use reasonable diplomacy and exercise care not to violate confidences. This type of functioning required the clinician to move through various roles as therapist, ombudsman, friendly visitor while remaining ready to aid his client in managing the stresses which tended to endanger psychological well being. The preventive nature of this kind of intervention was obvious.

And then there were the clients referred by the state mental hospital. They were our most difficult clients. They had been well "trained" in chronicity and we did not expect much in the way of stabilization. To attempt to maintain order for this difficult population and to bridge the conceptual professional gap with the hospital, one staff member was assigned to make regular visits to the major hospital serving the Program catchment area. Records of current patients were reviewed by this person and it was determined who would be living in our area. On these visits contacts would be made with patients not seen in the Program previously but who would be coming for aftercare. Also, former patients who had returned to the hospital would be contacted. In this manner the staff was alerted in an orderly fashion as to who should come to the clinic after release and when their medication would run out. Whenever necessary, follow-up visits were made if the patient failed to arrive.

During the visits to the hospital the staff was to try to form a relationship with the hospital staff. The attempts rarely succeeded. We were viewed as alien and an annoyance. My experience when I went was that interaction was minimally cordial, they would look up who was to be released, the records were dumped in a pile, and the nurse's station was evacuated by their staff.

Given the chronicity involved, therapy was typically not possible and the clinic typically handled medication needs. Yet, the staff attempted to monitor reality problems and visited clients' homes if they failed to make appointments. Whenever possible the staff tried to continue to oversee stress problems in their environment, advocated for them when necessary, and saw to it that they had a friendly place to come if only for coffee and a brief chat. Again, there was a preventive orientation and avoidance of hospitalizations was a clear money-saver not to mention the humane element.

Performing all these functions would have been much easier if the state hospital had been willing to share staff. If staff had been working at both the hospital and satellite, it would have been possible to follow people at the hospital, as outpatients, and to see them at home. Undoubtedly, the staff of the state hospital could have gained more understanding of their patients from the experiences of community mental health workers.

For example, there was an instance when I talked housing project personnel out of pressing for payment of a bill that a fundamentally psychotic woman claimed she did not owe. She was becoming quite agitated, and I feared a return to the hospital. At my insistence the project forgave the small bill and a week later I visited her at home, where she was in a relaxed mood and painting her apartment. It was worth it to all involved.

We will never know what reform of the system might have achieved. In the end the budgets of the hospitals were slashed and many of the people were turned out onto the streets where they roamed as our city homeless. The alternative might have been shrinking of the hospital system but with more effective follow-up and fewer hospitalizations needed even for the most chronic patients. All that is sheer conjecture, nonetheless.

But the major part of our work revolved around outpatient and related activities. Although walk-in clinic morning could be hectic for a clinician and mornings when medication was dispensed were sometimes crowded, the clinic usually looked quiet. Quiet prevailed because the services were organized in such a way that the clinic had more of an atmosphere of a private facility than an overcrowded poverty area clinic. Visitors could often not believe that the staff was busy or that they were in an impoverished area of a large city. They believed that a clinic in such an area should have "people hanging out the windows". It was simply not necessary. Since the clinical load was heavy, the staff was forced to review cases carefully and judiciously pace visits or concentrate on specific clients who could benefit the most. In practice, even during peak periods, it became a matter of efficiency and rarely was service to an individual client inadequate. After the initial visit, each patient had a regular appointment and once they learned that the staff would be prompt, they were usually on time. Thus the clients arrived shortly before their appointments, were ushered into an office, and left immediately after their appointments. In this way, although offices were filled, the building looked quiet.

Because the Western Satellite Center served an area approximately 50-50 Black and White there was from time to time a debate about the racial composition of the staff and how the clients were allocated. Our experience was that race simply did not matter much at all. The staff was mixed racially and received whoever came for walk-in clinic. Although an occasional client made a prejudiced remark within earshot, there seemed to be no significant reaction to the race of the clinician.

Soul-searching about racial attitudes at the beginning proved to be essential. It was important to be alert to prejudice on the part of the staff. We quickly became aware of the fact that we were all prejudiced and it extended to class prejudice as well as race. The staff did not play games about "calling out" prejudice in each other. We noted when we saw the effects of it and accepted the fact that prejudice is part of the human condition and represented the dark side of our social nature. Honest management was at issue, not the existence of prejudice.

The staff at the Western Satellite Center came to believe that the notion that Blacks should serve Blacks and Whites should serve Whites was totally inappropriate. In fact, in the city we encountered numerous examples of people who were prejudiced in one way or another against their own race. Or perhaps they simply

32

were disdainful of people from a lower socioeconomic status. In the end we took all comers and worked to manage the prejudices we knew we had.

CLIENT RESPONSE

Once the staff was clear about the general nature of the problems faced by their clients, it became easier to design services. Fundamentally, the pressures in the inner city made it inevitable that our clients would be crisis oriented. So, we had to be prepared to respond to crises.

Typical of intervention even when there were very serious problems was a woman who could not make progress in traditional psychotherapy. There had been two brief hospitalizations on the inpatient unit, and eventually she learned to call for an appointment when she was in crisis. Usually after two or three sessions during the crisis period, when I would be very directive, she would again be able to cope for another three to six months. It appeared that long-term hospitalization was prevented and she did not develop a more serious chronic condition. More enduring progress would have been desirable, but she was kept functioning.

Medication was also an issue. In many settings, too often it was the only assistance offered and many clients came expecting it. Certainly there were people who needed medication and benefited from it. But clients were not routinely referred for medication. In this regard we had to educate our clients and change the conditions of their expectations.

Again, University personnel warned us that our clients would be unreliable and would not come on time and frequently not show up at all. Staff experience as to frequency of return and general utilization of the serve was distinctly at variance from what we had been told to expect. Naturally, the client population included some very disturbed people and, given the nature of their distress, one would expect a certain percentage of the population to refuse service or to be markedly unreliable. Even for the more stable individuals there were issues of getting off from work, transportation problems, and such things as sudden illness among their children.

Unfortunately, during the early years of the Program there was no well-developed statistical report system which could supply feedback on appointments kept, appointments missed, whether they were canceled, or whether a request was made for another appointment. I kept some statistics for short periods which indicated that 75-80% of my appointments were kept and of the remaining 20-25% the majority of the clients called to cancel or arrange another appointment before, during, or shortly after the appointment time. Our experience generally did not suggest a pattern of irresponsible utilization of services.

Clients tended to be somewhat irregular in coming on time and keeping appointments at the beginning of therapy, but became more regular as therapy progressed. Although a strengthened relationship between client and worker would partly account for the change, it also related to their previous experiences at other clinics, where they could expect to be kept waiting for hours. Once they learned that the staff would be prompt, they tended to be prompt as well.

I will never forget the expression on the face of a young woman who was just beginning work with me. She stood in the waiting room with her mouth open and finally said, "You really are here waiting for me!" It was all about very simple human transactions.

In terms of punctuality, the clients were not punctual. Compulsivity was not a cardinal feature of the population we served and the staff found it undesirable to make an issue of their being a few minutes late. A few minutes one way or the other was not important to them. And, the bus might have been late.

It seemed distressingly obvious to our staff that when people were treated like cattle, they acted like cattle and when they were responded to as human beings, they responded to the indication of their personal worth. Clients availed themselves of services because the staff was willing to:

- Respond to the most relevant stresses in their lives, considering with them what was appropriate in order to work out a mutually agreeable plan in a realistic fashion relating to what were clear priorities and what they were willing to accept.
- Advocate for them with other systems and agencies.
- Reveal themselves as real people and treat the client the same.
- Make a contract on a crisis basis if that was what was necessary.

In this way the delivery of services was optimized. In short, the poor inner city residents can utilize mental health services and benefit from them when professionals act responsibly and appropriately. The job of professionals as we saw it was to intervene with clients and for clients in order to decrease stresses and prevent a deterioration of their mental condition. Clients derived benefits of improved functioning, less pain, and, although professionals might never get to some deep-seated personal problems, they could usually feel they had been of distinct benefit.

THE SOURCE OF REFERRAL

The sources of referrals changed over time from the opening of the clinic until it was an established organization. The source gave some indication of the motivation of the client, how well the client was prepared for utilizing services, and how the client would utilize services.

When the doors of the clinic were first opened for services, a large number of referrals came from the Department of Social Services. These initial referrals were not chronic psychotic cases on the whole but included chronic cases of inadequate personality, depression, and psychosomatic illness. They had not been successfully treated elsewhere and were now being referred to a new resource.

Unfortunately, they were generally not prepared well by the people making the referrals, and many came not even knowing the name of the facility but simply having been given an address to which they were to go. Often when they realized the nature of the facility, they became quite resistant to accepting treatment. Such a beginning did little for the morale of the staff and tended to confirm the notion that the poor will not come and cannot benefit from services. It became clear that this segment of the population represented a troublesome group of people for the welfare workers. Because they were troublesome, they took priority in making referrals over those already receiving treatment which might be inadequate to their needs and those persons in early stages of the development of mental illness.

In the early days the people referred by agencies were in no way representative of the population at large either in regard to those needing or not needing service. This occurrence demonstrated the need to educate the personnel of other agencies as to who could benefit from services, what services were offered, and how to prepare a client to receive and accept services. Without getting ahead of ourselves, it must be said that this truly was a valid consultation and education service as we educated other professionals on how to use us.

It was surprising how many welfare workers felt that the clinic staff might be able to work some magic if they could at least get their client in the door, even though the client was relatively unmotivated, possibly having sunk into hopelessness. It was obvious to us that nobody was further ahead by them refusing services at the facility than to never have come at all.

Once services were established, the state mental hospital began to send clients. These people were long-term chronic cases who tended to cycle in and out of the hospital. Little could be done for most of them and they became known to the staff as "maintenance cases". After initial assessment, an attempt was made to "dezom-bify" them somewhat by lowering the dose of medication. This was in the early days of the use of psychotropic medications; there were few options and consider-ably less knowledge.

Next, an assessment was made of the environmental problems they faced that might require assistance. In the event that they did not return for their appointments for medication, which was common, a home visit was made and an attempt was made to continue a relationship.

Clearly we were dealing with very different populations. The state hospital population was well entrenched and, in addition to their intrinsic problems, they had been well trained in chronicity. The balance of our clients had no experience with real helping relationships aside from the occasional dedicated social services worker. We had to open a whole new world to them.

Once again we were confronted with triage types of approaches. The state hos-pital population could have simply submerged our services in a sea of repetitious interventions, leaving little time for other work. We had to make efforts, we had to be efficient, and we had to know when to quit.

For purposes of economy of time, it was necessary to make visits to the clinic serve two purposes. Each regular clinical staff member accepted some of these people on his or her caseload. When they came to see the psychiatric consultant for medication, patients also visited with the staff member assigned to their case. In this fashion it was possible to continue to monitor their progress and continue to help with problems as they arose. These visits became therapeutic in the sense of having someone friendly to talk to even if it did not lead to much of anywhere in terms of ameliorating their problems. Although it cannot be proven, there was the feeling that this kind of monitoring and intervention tended to decrease the fre-quency with which they returned to the hospital.

As the clinic became better known in the area, there was a steady increase in the number of referrals from the best referral sources of all - former patients, friends, relatives, and neighbors. When people came for service at the suggestion of these individuals, they usually were well motivated for service and had reasonable knowl-edge of what could be expected to happen. Thus, there was less of a problem in formulating an effective approach. These referrals were often made to a particular staff member who was trusted, rather than to the facility. Even when I felt I had not been particularly effective with a person as a therapist, that person continued to make referrals because the trust issue was paramount. This experience was similar for the entire staff of the unit once they became established and known in the community. Thus, the attachment was less to a facility and more to a particular trusted individual. In cases where the former therapist had left the Program, it was generally possible to make arrangements to have the new patient accept another therapist. There seemed to be sufficient generalization of trust to permit someone else to take the case.

Looking back, it seems to me that it took at least eighteen months for the clinic to become well enough established to perceive a steady growth in referrals directly from the community. It took this long in spite of tremendous need, in part, at least, because the problem of trust was large and people tended to seek help from clinics and institutions only as a last resort and would go first to family or friends. This pattern began to be broken when word of mouth indicated that the clinic staff would work hard on their behalf.

THERAPIST ORIENTATIONS AND INPUT

It is worth noting again that these experiences took place in the late 1960s, barely twenty years after the end of World War II. Training still emphasized classical psychotherapeutic intervention, and psychoanalysis was still in vogue at least for a limited slice of the population.

Then came a major reform movement, the Poverty Program, and community mental health. Mental health services were no longer to be for the elite but extended to all people. That meant that we had to design new forms of services. Focusing on resistance, defenses, peeling the onion, transference, being a blank screen - all had to be reevaluated.

In the inner city the first move was to make the clinician a real human being to his or her clients. Professional distance of some kind had to be maintained, but it badly needed modification. It took a lot of learning for the staff to figure out what the modifications meant. There were long discussions and debates. Hard guidelines were not available, and intuition was often relied upon until we became conversant with a new form of functioning.

We could see at once that our clients had come to mistrust agency personnel who often did damaging things "in the best interest of the client". It was hard to overcome mistrust when the clinician was wholly withholding of their own humanity.

The damage done by some agency personnel was wholly understandable. Jobs in inner city agencies were much sought after by the local population. They meant a step up, but the reality was that they were hard to maintain as a lifetime career.

Burning out was a continuing problem. The assault of a seemingly endless line of traumatized inner city residents was hard to endure.

In response, some workers would pull into a callous shell and became the consummate bureaucrat. Others constantly increased their efforts, personal involvement and level of compassion until they were unable to sustain themselves and they had to leave. And then there were the ones who turned on their clients. They blamed the victim. There were many variations of these symptoms of burn out and they, along with damaging attitudes of professionals, contributed heavily to a climate that worked against productively taking part in services. In fact, many of the workers were just as trapped as the other inner city residents. They had nowhere else to go for a job.

In the case of our clinicians, it was essential to assume different roles. They might be exceedingly quiet when engaged in sessions which were more classically "therapeutic" but move swiftly to advocacy, guidance, and even a strong directive approach. Sometimes it was necessary to express strong opinions. In short, they were performing much more as a total human being and often had to put aside the mantle of the omnipotent therapist.

At the same time the therapist was moving from role to role even as he had to maintain a consistent self. Attempts to become like the client, including use of slang or colloquial expressions which were not natural were perceived as phony by the client and generally marked the green and naive staffer. Being on their side and working with and for them did not necessarily mean wearing blue jeans and a sweatshirt. In fact, all clothing options were possible even in those days when clothing was more formal.

The clients had to feel that they were dealing with someone genuine who was giving his or her best. Just as adolescents need parents and not more older friends, the inner city resident needed someone to confide in and to help them who was professional yet not a stuffed shirt. It was not a posture easily learned.

Therapeutic relationships came in many forms and even though the clinician might assume the role of a home visitor, guide, or stern parent, transference often developed anyway. Respect ran both ways. It was impossible not to respect the monumental strengths of many of these people who labored in a difficult environment. Support came in many forms but rarely in an ongoing sympathetic position, which we found tended to support long term dysfunction. There were times when we would express direct opinions and, at times, get angry. Priorities had to be set and acted on, often at once.

INTERPRETATIONS

It was necessary to broaden the meaning of interpretations. There were times when something was emerging along classical lines of psychotherapy but interpretations often graded off into direct reflections on reality and how effective the client's functioning was.

When it was clear reality that had to be dealt with, the time for interpretation might be that moment. In the classical sense, the manner and timing of the interpretation would be important.

And then there were surprises when an unsophisticated person began to speak in ways and demonstrated behaviors which seemed to reveal deep-seated symbolic material. Yet, their unsophisticated nature always had to be taken into account. Making the wrong move and making it too soon might lead the person to feel that the clinician was "putting him on" or making fun of him, creating distance. Usually it was essential to have a view in a reality context.

THE PROBLEM FOR WOMEN

This was the era when the most modern form of women's liberation was beginning. And it is difficult to find a population of women more in need of liberation. Life was a struggle, a partner essential and too often lacking.

In general the women were trapped in a struggle with men. The women from Appalachia often took the position of having to "stand by her man" in the words of the classic country song of the time. That meant putting up with a lot.

Black women were no more fortunate. Good stable men in an unstable environment were hard to find. As with anyone, the women wanted partnership, love, affection and support.

Regardless of race, if a woman asserted herself she might suffer the most grievous consequences. People who were most in need of liberation were the least likely to get it.

While at times it was possible to raise a woman's consciousness enough to work out a better relationship with fewer hurtful elements, mobilizing too much outrage at her circumstances could prove ruinous. Intervention had to be done with care, attending to the harsh realities of her existence.

INSIGHT CAN BE BAD

It was obvious that much of the work with clients had to do not with intrapsychic phenomena as much as environmental or life stress. In that case it was often justifiable to avoid insight in the sense of coldly facing the impact of their troubles and stresses. Suppression and repression in the inner city environment were adaptive responses when people were dealing with problems beyond their control. Insight could be tantamount to demonstrating the hopelessness of the situation.

For example, a man came complaining of "nervousness". He was working to support his wife and ten children and was underemployed, had not finished high school, and had not learned about training programs which might improve his economic situation. The family was strained severely by raising so many young children and by their marginal economic condition. He knew a lot of other men who had fled their large families, and he wrestled with the desire to flee himself. However, he felt a sense of obligation and genuinely cared for his wife, with whom he could not spend enough time. There were many more difficult years ahead.

No doubt there was anger about his situation and nowhere to direct it. He had suffered emotional damage in his family of origin, and the related deprivation made his current circumstances feel worse. He tried desperately not to think of the years ahead. Insight would have meant looking at an approach-avoidance conflict for which he felt he could find no solution. His "nervousness" was increasing, and he was showing a pattern of leaving and returning to his family.

The obvious solution was to seek an improvement in the economic welfare of the family, as well as dealing with concurrent physical health problems. A review of the family problems was in order, to give the client a clearer view, not of the situation but of what could be done to ameliorate it. A total review in the context of a helpful partnership was in order, and, in fact, it was possible to get training with supporting funds, which later had the effect of improving the family's situation considerably. Attending to the children's physical health issues relieved other burdens. In the end the well-being of the family was improved with eventual considerable improvement in his feelings of well-being.

VOCATIONAL REHABILITATION

One other crucial piece of the services must be mentioned. Poverty is a central issue in the inner city and unemployment or underemployment was pervasive.

Each satellite center had a counselor from the Division of Vocational Rehabilitation (DVR). We considered for each and every client whether there was a role for a referral to DVR. We simply had to establish a diagnosis to make the client eligible, and we were flexible about it. A simple, uncomplicated diagnosis opened doors for medical services, training, and education. It was directed at giving clients a viable vocational future. The success stories were wonderful to see and hear. Depressed welfare recipients became wage earners who could see a brighter future for their family.

One service that was fruitful for a time was training women whose marriages had ended and who were economically stranded without skills. We were able to rehabilitate these women and provide the skills for gainful employment. They became wage earners and taxpayers.

Unfortunately, in later years DVR lost its way. To defend their funding they turned to a focus on the severely disabled which all too often meant making commitments of resources to chronic mental illness sufferers, with whom there was little hope of having a major impact. With the diversion of funds to persons with severe chronic disabilities, the funds for training women to be employable were no longer available.

TOTAL MANAGEMENT AND MISMANAGEMENT

At the time, studies of the effectiveness of psychotherapy were just beginning, and early on it was assumed that therapy could do no harm. The issues already highlighted suggested that therapists could, in fact, do considerable harm.

The application of the medical model could lead the clinician in the wrong direction with the wrong tools. We learned that total management was the essential approach. Developmental issues might be important, but so were current stresses in the environment - and in the case of the inner city resident were generally paramount.

Following is an example of a supreme malfunction of helping systems.

A woman I shall call Phelanee was one of my earliest cases in the inner city. Many of the details of her history and existence are relatively unimportant in this context except for a few facts.

Her childhood was a horror story of mistreatment, constant moves, and fear for her own well-being. Her early marriage merely continued the previous conditions, with her violent and dangerous husband threatening her with a gun while he sat drinking and forced her to sit in front of him.

Whatever Happened to Community Mental Health?

When she came to the clinic she was markedly depressed, suicidal, on welfare, and abused drugs occasionally. The necessary environmental interventions were made on a continuing basis but it was necessary and desirable to engage in long-term psychotherapy. Some initial dramatic improvement appeared to enable her to overcome a dangerous suicidal period.

An early visit to her apartment in the projects revealed a neat and well-ordered home and three children with intelligence shining brightly in their eyes. They were playing quietly and viewed me, the intruder, cautiously. It was apparent that they watched over their mother, but it was clear that they were also pursuing their own lives as children. Seeing them gave me a sense of hope.

Her personal life improved with intervention, but it was not possible for her to leave her environment and move beyond her welfare status. She continued in periodic but less dangerous crises that required repeated incursions into insight-oriented therapy. But clearly a plateau was reached after the initial period. She was coping better but barely managing to maintain herself and her family in the dangerous environment of the projects.

She had lived in the projects for many years and was well liked by project staff and her long-term neighbors. Over time she needed less and less frequent intervention. Unbeknownst to me, however, she began to experience harassment by new neighbors who brought with them an all too common hostility toward people known to be "mental cases". With time on their hands, it was not uncommon for them to stir up excitement by harassing such lonely individuals.

After not seeing her for a while, I received a call from an emergency room in the nearest hospital where she had been taken with a mild overdose of tranquilizers. It was not a serious suicide attempt but indicated a plea for assistance. It seemed that harassment had continued to increase, and she felt helpless against it. The harassment included anonymous tips to the police suggesting that she was dealing drugs. In turn there was constant surveillance of her apartment, and at one point she found her apartment surrounded by police while her preteen daughter was having a party. She became furious and finally depressed. Her condition was deteriorating.

She improved after a brief hospitalization on the inpatient unit while the machinations of her neighbors were directed elsewhere in her absence. Pathological elements were hardening and she insisted, despite her weak condition, that she wanted another child. She had a history of serious problems during pregnancies and this desire was fairly self-destructive but she would not be dissuaded. She had never carried a child to full term and of eight pregnancies had only three living children.

Her pregnancy was difficult from the beginning and she made the mistake of seeking care at a hospital where she was not known. Her previous experiences with hospitals included being accused of having an illegal abortion when she came to one emergency room while miscarrying. They refused treatment while she was badgered by emergency room personnel and the police. Someone finally reached a friendly physician who knew her history and was successful in getting her proper medical assistance. In view of this incident and numerous other kinds of mistreatment by medical personnel, she was justifiably fearful.

Naturally we discussed the self-destructive nature of the pregnancy in view of her past experiences. The key point here, however, is what then ensued in the name of medical management.

The physicians responsible for her physical care during her pregnancy saw their job as exclusively relating to achieving a full-term pregnancy. They utterly ignored her emotional condition and treated her physical condition in isolation. This meant that when she had premature labor pains she was removed to the hospital and placed in the labor room until the doctors were assured labor was stopped. Having been in a labor room with my wife when our second child was born, I saw it as a barbarous place for a vulnerable woman alone with no one to support or succor her. This woman with a history of suicide attempts was subjected to lonely pain while she had nothing more to do than dwell upon her fears for her unborn child and listen to the lonely agonies of the women around her.

After her release from the hospital she was less and less able to move from her bed, but except for trips to the hospital, which depressed her seriously, she seemed to manage reasonably well. As her pregnancy came to term the welfare department made a series of errors with her check and claimed they could not find a way to make arrangements for the care of her children. Repeated interventions on my part finally succeeded in forcing a reasonable response.

Her depression was increasing and the "responsible" physician repeated that his only job was to bring the child to term and refused to face any of the ramifications of her other problems. A brief hospitalization was arranged on our inpatient unit in the middle of her last month.

When she came to term there was an infuriating exchange with another hospital, which had received prepayment for the delivery. They insisted that they would not permit the hospital where she was an inpatient to perform the delivery and would not forward payment. No sympathetic psychiatric personnel could be on hand, and there was a midnight dash across town to the other hospital where she gratefully gave birth to a healthy daughter.

I left the program shortly after the birth of this child. I later learned that her condition had steadily worsened and she had begun using heroin.

Was this the inevitable outcome for her? What stood out to me was that this woman was assaulted daily by events in her environment. I had come to know a woman who was intelligent and adaptable in many ways. She had nurtured her children well in spite of her problems and I believed that somehow their lives would be better than hers. But the effect of the sum of personal and environmental issues were too much for her. Repeatedly such experiences led the staff of the program to focus ever more strongly on the particular system designed to help the people of the area.

A BROAD BASED APPROACH

Without doubt the foregoing case of Phelanee indicated that traditional psychotherapy was not the primary treatment of choice. History alone as it affects the psychological well-being of a person was far from the only issue. In many cases deep-rooted personal issues might be at play but so might current reality factors. The clinician had to decide what intervention was most important and most effective.

During an intake interview it was always desirable to obtain a history and to assess important areas of functioning reflective of real-life issues. But the information gathered was of no importance if no relationship was formed. And in very many of the clients the reality issues and help with them were the keys to the relationship. As each problem was solved, the client became less distressed and together client and therapist could decide what to focus on next.

There was no way to predict with a high degree of certainty what problems might be presented in the first interview. The clinician had to be prepared to move in any number of directions.

At the time, interview schedules were in vogue. But in the inner city environment spontaneity was essential along with broad-ranging intervention. Standard formats or institutional rigidity were impediments to effective work. The client may have held the keys, but the clinician had to help them decide what keys to use.

It was also essential to take the approach of going to the world of the client and working from there. It was important to understand the cultural climate of the client. Whether the client's culture was that of Appalachia or the Deep South was important. And sometimes there were serious unanticipated effects.

Over time I developed a strong relationship with the personnel working in the projects. In one instance they had called in a psychiatrist to assess a seriously disturbed and disturbing woman. He declared her to be a paranoid schizophrenic in need of immediate hospitalization. Instead, one of the workers called me.

The woman had moved to Baltimore from an isolated rural area of South Carolina where she had grown up the child of Haitian immigrants. She began to tell me a story which seemed disconnected but had a thread of magic. Finally, to back up her story, she told me of finding indications of spells left on her doorstep, and with a little probing revealed that she believed she was the object of a voodoo practitioner. From the project staff I learned there was indeed another woman from a similar culture who had taken a particular dislike to this woman.

The intervention was crystal clear. There was nothing psychotic about a culture-consistent belief system. By good fortune we were able to move her to another project virtually at once and away from the machinations of the practitioner she feared so much. Not surprisingly her condition improved dramatically without medication and without a hospitalization.

Add to the intrapsychic assessment the effects of reality issues and an assessment of cultural effects when at all possible, and the clinician brings powerful tools to the work. We will see later how effective this mix is even outside of the inner city.

CONCLUSION

Together with the assumption of normalcy, the staff had to assume that service might be blocked or made ineffective because of prior negative experiences in seeking help. Prior experiences may have conditioned some clients to assume both that they would be devalued and that they would be given medication. Sometimes medication was necessary as a temporary matter, but generally other forms of intervention were preferred initially.

Clients in this type of setting did not come with a high degree of sophistication and had to be educated in the use of psychotherapy, if it was even indicated after a reality-based approach was used. Trust was a primary issue and an honest approach was essential whereby the clinician presented himself as a "genuine person" while maintaining appropriate distance.

"Curing" the client was generally not a primary goal, because the real cure would be found in the environment. Maximizing effective coping skills, providing resources, and removing stresses were essential.

It was important to impress upon new staff members the need to be careful not to devalue the client . The staff had to look beyond social class, race, sex, appearance, and culture, among other things. Attending to these differences moved the clinician beyond traditional training. There was nothing mysterious about this approach. It responded to the context and the needs of a particular client group.

Chapter 3
Consultation to Community Agencies

CONTEXT

There are ideals and there are realities. Young professionals have to respond to the charge they are given. Training in an academic setting sets some responses. But then, in the inner city, there is a harsh reality and the setting in which they must function can be unforgiving. They leave the office with resolve, charged to become consultants and walk into an alien landscape with real people and find they are on their own. Do they fall back on training or rely on themselves and "instincts"? Fundamentally there is no escaping the fact that there is a job to do and the best advice is to face the fact and learn to cope - at times all alone.

Mental health professionals will spend most of their time delivering services on a one-to-one basis. Although psychiatric personnel have often engaged in consulting types of activities, at the time it generally was not seen as a primary job function either in the private or public spheres. Faced with this kind of new endeavor there came a time, at least at the beginning, when it was hard to know whether to fall on the floor and laugh or just burst into tears.

Gradually the argument began to be advanced that the mental health professional was largely wasting his time treating individuals when factors such as institutional policies, economics, social policy, etc. that affect the general incidence of mental illness were more properly the primary focus of his job.

The foremost work advancing this viewpoint was Gerald Caplan's *Principles of Preventive Psychiatry*. He presented an excellent case for emphasizing preventive types of consultation, from personal, political, and economic viewpoints.

The mental health professions by that time had acquired a great deal of knowledge about how to optimize human functioning in a wide variety of settings. In the decades since the publication of Caplan's work, the knowledge base has continued to expand rapidly, along with the sophistication of the population at large. Moreover, there are ways to affect the incidence of mental illness by dealing with larger factors. And, even with a strong societal commitment, there may be a shortage of mental health personnel.

Dr. Caplan's arguments fully accounted for the difficulty inherent in doing consultation. He recognized the limitations of consultation as well as the time needed to develop a reasonable relationship with the consultee. It is worthwhile to present the general points of his model.

Primary Prevention

The Caplan model for primary prevention was based on public health principles and involved attention to factors that may lower the rate of new cases of all kinds of mental illnesses in the target population over a period of time. Attention is focused on counteracting harmful policies, situations, and circumstances before they can produce mental illness. The activity is aimed at the population and not the individual. The acceptance of wider responsibility in a program of primary prevention means, for example, that poverty is seen as a target problem because the stresses and the complex variables involved in being poor are important in generating mental illness. His positions struck at core perceptions which structured the service delivery system in the inner city.

In seeking to undertake primary prevention Dr. Caplan saw mental health professionals as attending to the provision of "supplies" to the members of the target population. These supplies may be:

- Physical (food, shelter, sensory stimulation, opportunities for employment, recreation etc.);
- Psychosocial (involving provisions for cognitive and affective development through interactions within the family, peers, schools, on the job, and all aspects of the social environment); or
- Sociocultural (influences on the person's development which are seen in the customs and values of the culture and the structure of society).

The professional is seen as attending to the nature and significance of life crises including the characteristics of the crises, factors influencing the crisis resolution, sociocultural influences on crisis resolution, influences of the family, influence of significant others in the person's field of interaction, and the influence of the involved professional workers.

48

Attention to these factors in primary prevention leads the professional out of his office and into activities usually seen as being related to civic and social duty. In Caplan's view, it is legitimate for the professional to engage in social action to assist in changing conditions inimical to the mental health of most members of the focal population. In addition to broad programs of social action and the support of national policies viewed as promoting mental health, there would be attention to hazardous circumstances in specific crises, face-to-face interaction with individuals or small groups, mediation with other care-givers, etc. In short, intervention is made or support given to foster favorable conditions in the community to promote mental health.

Secondary Prevention

Inasmuch as mental health professionals cannot prevent all disorders, they must also turn their attention to lowering the rate of disability due to certain illnesses by lowering the rate of prevalence. This can be by altering the factors leading to the disorder (primary prevention) or through shortening the duration of existing cases through early case finding and effective treatment (secondary prevention). Thus, an attempt is made to identify persons in the early stages of an illness and get them into effective treatment as quickly as possible. This kind of work may involve improving diagnostic tools, early referral (often through education of the community and other caregivers, etc.), screening programs (as might be used to identify cases of brain damage where the effects may eventually lead to mental illness, either because of physical effects or psychological outcomes), or management of disorders in new ways (as in classes for disturbed children where "treatment" in a traditional sense is not undertaken).

It should be kept in mind that although these seem like discrete categories of prevention, there is substantial overlap and a professional may be doing all at once in some circumstances.

Tertiary Prevention

The third category of prevention is tertiary. In this case, the aim is to reduce the rate of defective functioning resulting from the mental illness. Tertiary prevention involves attempting to reduce residual effects by, for example, combating community prejudice against the mentally ill, shortening hospital stays, overcoming the patients' feelings of alienation, opening transitional institutions such as halfway houses, improving job opportunities through vocational rehabilitation, etc. Thus, even this category goes well beyond the scope of individual psychotherapy. The effects reach considerably beyond office treatment.

Caplan also outlined several types of consultation that might apply in certain cases:

- Client-centered case consultation;
- Program-centered administrative consultation;
- Consultee-centered consultation focusing on such thing as lack of skill, lack of objectivity, and lack of confidence and self-esteem; and
- Consultee-centered administrative consultation.

None of these types of consultation are, of course, likely to be pure types. A consultation can focus on issues of dealing with a particular case and its management while advising the consultee on his own functioning.

Caplan also outlined five phases of consultation;

- Preparing the ground for consultation
- The development of the individual consultation relationship
- Assessing the consultation problem
- The consultation message
- The ending and follow-up phase.

He cautioned that these phases may vary considerably in length of time and may involve months or even years. Thus, the writings of Caplan reframe consultation as a function in which the role of the professional is expanded well beyond treatment of individual patients. His message has much merit; it points out to the professional that prevention can be more important than treatment and it offers a way to spread effects more efficiently. Thus, the basic goal of the consultant is to prevent mental illness through a variety of means and thereby prevent the need for substantial work with mentally ill persons who need not have become ill. It can be seen how Caplan's thinking infiltrated every element of the design of our services in the inner city Program.

But in order to become an effective consultant, the professional must be aware of the goals to which he or she must aspire upon entering the world to act as a consultant. Caplan provides a pure, professional view, but my experience led me to identify the existence of many goals other than the kinds he mentions.

Roger B. Burt

COLD, HARD REALITY

In the early days of the program Caplan's book was the bible of the staff. Much of what he said had the ring of reality in the inner city. There were layers of interventions required which often involved various kinds of preventive work.

But often it seemed that many professionals viewed his thoughts as validating a perspective that mental health professionals could instill wisdom into other agencies. There was a grandiosity about some of the expectations.

When reality intruded it was harsh and cold. One of the first things given to me was a listing of all agencies in the city and descriptions of the services they offered. It was wondrous to behold.

There was only one problem. Many of them did not function as described or had meager resources for a beleaguered staff to deliver. Over time we had to discover, with some difficulty, what was or was not available. Meeting with an agency representative typically had the characteristics of a public relations activity. And sending a fragile client for services was not a good way to assess services that might not exist.

And so we hit the streets and talked to all manner of people in agencies and programs and on the streets. We gathered information about what their experiences had been and whom they knew. Relationships and networks were established. In time we had the view we needed, and it was disappointing. The art of the possible was developed.

One example well illustrates what we found. An obvious place to begin to get referrals for service and to give consultation was in the projects. And so we went to a management office in a high-rise project and knocked on their locked door. A frightened looking woman cracked the door and asked who we were and what we wanted.

We learned that the management staff in the projects had a mission. They were to be available to the residents to help them get education and find the programs that they needed, with the goal of preparing them for a better life and future. In time they could leave the inner city and poverty behind. It sounded familiar to us.

But what they told us was that each day was a battle for them. They received a constant stream of complaints about everything from a resident who simply threw diapers and trash out of her window to chronically broken elevators. Pools of urine stood in stairways and the physical structure itself seemed under attack.

51

In short, they needed help and felt besieged. In time we were able to form a viable relationship and sort out where we could or could not be of help. The project staff generally felt inadequate to assess the real problem suffered by a given person or how to sort it out. Sometimes we could help and often we undertook home visits to do the assessment.

It was impossible to know what lay behind the door we would knock on.

In one instance they asked me to assess a woman whom they billed as the "original welfare recipient". She was troublesome and to other residents an object of fear.

I found her seated regally in a chair in the center of her living room. She seemed amused by my visit, and she had probably had many such visitors. Shortly she deftly let her housecoat fall open to reveal her breasts. Not getting a reaction, or the one she wanted, she wrapped herself up again and we finished the interview.

There were young women coming and going, and she referred to them as her daughters. Occasionally a young child wandered in and out. It did not take much to see that her "daughters" were prostitutes and she was the madam. No doubt drugs were flowing through the apartment as well.

Needless to say, the office management was not surprised. The welfare department was not interested in being involved because there was never any cooperation and they already had much more than they could possibly do. The police were similarly unenthusiastic about involvement in a small time prostitution operation. If arrested they would all be back in the apartment almost immediately.

And so we talked about a policy of containment with just enough intervention to decrease disturbance and to make them careful about how they affected their neighbors. It wasn't much of an intervention but the management staff seemed happy with the plan. Over time we received an increasing number of valid referrals.

Probably our best consultation relationship was with the Community Action Agency. They had a constant stream of people coming into their offices and had developed roots in the community they served. Their staff soon came to see us as allies and a genuine resource. We had to be careful not to put up barriers and demonstrated what we could and could not do. But especially we made it clear that we were there to help and were not making pronouncements from a lofty perch. Eagerly they invited us on home visits and helped us build an image in the community, which in turn led to more valid referrals.

And so we learned by doing. We heard what Caplan said and saw a certain validity. But his words were spoken a long way from the gritty streets of inner city Baltimore.

GOALS FOR CONSULTATION

In any intense environment, whether it is an emergency room, a war zone, or the inner city, dark humor on the part of the staff is a lifeline. We talked about goals for consultation that Caplan did not mention. Any reader who is working or has worked in an agency, will have observed many of the following goals. Forgive my cynicism.

They fell broadly into four groups: 1. Professional Goals; 2. Status Goals; 3. Ego Goals; and 4. Escape Goals.

1. Professional Goals:
   - To Write Professional Papers - Clinical settings do not lend themselves to detailed research but real or imagined consultation successes make good copy.
   - Expansion of the Curriculum Vitae - Carefully framed consultation activities can look good on paper. A long, slow and dogged development of a relationship is not glamorous.
2. Status Goals:
   - Enhancement of Status - At least at the time, being a consultant enhanced status more than an arduous, diverse work schedule.
   - Becoming Widely Known - Being known to many agencies spreads fame and recognition. There were professionals who were gadflies flitting from one agency to another.
   - Gaining Power - Simply put, power attends the mystique of the busy consultant.
   - Money - Status Enhancement - Smoothly political consultants appeared to get good promotions and the money that went with it.
   - Building an Entourage - The arrival of a consultant with an entourage is a dynamic experience and a welcome diversion from dreary employment.
3. Ego Goals: The staff had fun identifying the goals they saw and could see that the goals in this section were closely related to status but had a slightly different function in enhancing feelings of self worth.
   - Glamour - It is simply true that being a consultant implies glamour.
   - Demonstration of Abilities - There was ample opportunity to observe consultants at work in agencies. Some engaged in dazzling displays of in-depth psychological analyses delivered to hapless employees required to attend by their superiors. Often they ended with well-constructed recommendations for activities. Generally they could not hope to be implemented for lack of

resources. But the consultant could take satisfaction in his triumph and his self-worth was enhanced.

- Reinforcing Omniscience - A consultant is supposedly a consultant because of superior knowledge. The larger the ego, the more the meetings were designed to reinforce his omniscience.
- Mutual Admiration - It may be time off from an arduous day and a welcome break and the meeting may turn into a mutual admiration society or it may be alternatively called a folie a deux.
- Talking to Themselves - When the consultation is with and among the personnel composing the upper echelon of the agency, difficult issues can be avoided and successes may be hailed. The most cynical staff called it mental masturbation. It also served to firm up territorial boundaries.
- Socializing - There is nothing complex about it. The meeting may be nothing other than a social hour.
- Insensitive "Sensitivity Training" - Sensitivity training was in vogue at the time and almost every staff member had been subjected to it. Too often an incompetent or mischievous trainer did damage. Our environment was fraught with cultural, racial, and sexual traps. The dance we had to do was best done to the rhythms of daily interactions, not by fiat. The staff was adamant. There would be no sensitivity training.
- Destroying Another Agency - It didn't happen often but on occasions someone would seek power and use it to play out a vendetta or bias. It is very easy to play on the skeletons and stresses of an agency. It is always easy to do damage and more difficult to make a truly positive contribution.

4. Escape Goals - The work was draining in a difficult setting. Burn out rates for staff were high. Getting away from it all was crucial. While we hoped it was productive, sometimes it was just desirable to get away from the office.

- Free time - Since consulting relationships take time to develop and often friendships develop among like-minded people, it is a perfect opportunity to have some free time in a relaxing environment.
- Treatment of Depression - People in the armed services get R & R and clinical staff needs it too within the work day. It is good for their mental health. Increased chatter about primary prevention and consultation was a sure warning sign.
- Get Away from Poor People - Our clients were important to us and we were dedicated, but sometimes enough was enough. Our clients might not have the option of a consultation assignment, but we did.

GOALS FOR THE CONSULTEE

Naturally we saw that goals were not confined to the consultant. The consultee also had goals. The art was found in pleasing both parties.

1. Professional Goals -
   - Pleasing the Higher Ups - It can't hurt to please the boss. If the boss arranges the consultation, the staff has to look at the real goal. Or they may arrange for the consultation, which may make them seem forward looking with a breadth of vision.
   - Forcing Out Unwanted Staff - Particularly in state agencies, getting rid of unwanted staff is difficult. Making them want to leave is often faster, and one way to achieve that is putting them into consultation experiences that will make them uncomfortable or make them appear incompetent.
   - Covering Inadequacies - The mere existence of consultation activities gives the impression of an active and adaptive organization.
   - Block Out Other Consultants - Having a consultant obviates the need for other ones, or at least that argument can be advanced. Either the agency has a defense or may have someone who genuinely helps.
2. Status Goals -
   - Enhancement by Length of Consultant List - Having a lengthy list of consultants makes an agency look good. The reality of what is actually happening may be another matter entirely.
   - Increased Control of Staff - How this works depends upon the type of alliance built between the consultant and the person doing the hiring. The goal may be legitimate and positive or negative, depending on power and control issues.
3. Ego Goals -
   - Mutual Back Scratching - This relates to the mutual admiration society mentioned above but is from the agency's view. The consultant spends time reinforcing what a wonderful job the agency is doing and the staff in turn praises the consultation efforts.
   - Get the Boss - If the agency staff members are unhappy with the senior agency staff, they can spend their time underscoring the problems with the head of the agency.
   - Proving the Consultant Wrong - The most common form of resistance was seen in continually bringing up inappropriate or hopeless cases with strong

pleas for service. People engaging in this type of resistance or sabotage were commonly the agency "bleeding hearts" with considerable underlying hostility and passive-aggressive skills. The consultant was labelled as someone who truly did not wish to serve the poor, unfortunate client.

4. Escape Goals -
   * Getting Out of Work - The possibilities are endless, and staff moves to bring up endless make-work projects to prevent them from getting to what is difficult or distasteful.
   * Inviting Other Agencies - The suggestion of bringing other agencies into the consultation may seem innocent enough, but it can be in the service of avoiding constructive activities. The burden of work to control the process falls to the consultant who will find it difficult to get to meaningful issues. Constantly bringing in new people means the new people have to be "brought up to speed" and that consumes a great deal of time.

BEING A NONCONSULTANT

It is apparent that as a corollary to Murphy's Law there are more ways for consultation to go wrong than there are for it to go right. Our staff over time saw all of the problems listed above, and the most useful purpose of consultation was to show them how not to engage in consultation. In fact, seeing negative examples may often be more instructive than seeing effective examples that make it look easy.

The pitfalls were numerous, and dysfunctional consultation was obviously something to be avoided. Therefore, interactions with other agencies needed to be a focus of staff discussion and supervision. Such supervision required more attention than day-to-day interventions with clients.

The length of time consultation activities at a given agency had been going on was often not seen as an issue. It took a very long time to gain trust, get to know the personalities involved, understand the true workings of the agency and develop a truly useful relationship.

RECEIVING CONSULTATION

Although giving consultation was one of the five essential services, our staff was not immune to receiving such services. But there was a twist. Community mental health as constructed was a new endeavor and truly experienced consultants who had worked in such settings were few and far between.

When it was announced that we were to have consultation regarding our services, it was usually greeted with groans. Most of the consultants came with academic viewpoints and few had actually worked in this kind of inner city setting.

We politely sat through lectures that had no bearing on what we actually encountered. The consultants were generally idealistic, well intentioned and were often romantics.

At times there were moments of high comedy. Often a tour of our area was indicated, and we went out onto the streets to show the consultants our work environment.

One of my favorite days was when I was escorting a man from NIMH. He stopped by a trash-filled alley and waxed eloquent about the romance attached to viewing the disorder and heaps of trash. He saw an essential beauty and touching pathos.

Just down the street we came upon one of my favorite skilled junkies. He was invariably clean and decently dressed which inspired confidence on the part of his targets. I referred to him as having a finely honed "rap".

This "poor" man had supposedly been the victim of a street robbery. His wife and a child were ill, at an emergency room across town, and he was desperate for cab fare to get to them. In this fashion he sought to get more than pocket change and was often successful. It was hard not to take pity on him.

I stood there torn between the adoration of romance in an inner city alley and a great performance by a talented man feeding his drug habit.

Meetings were often a bizarre combination of feigning interest and approval of the consultant and covering for the misdeeds of the University and State when funds were misdirected. We often could not speak to the real nature of our work or how the service delivery actually worked. We had work to do, and the visits were nothing more than a diversion.

The overall situation seems, in retrospect, absurdly clear. We were viewed as a group of inexperienced "kids" with good intentions but in need of guidance. Our view was that we were learning fast and had to develop services while being, supervised by people who had little interest in what we were doing. We saw them as often grandiose, venal, and more interested in protecting their territory and status than in getting the job done. From my view decades later, the "kids" saw reality.

The lesson for my life was to take nothing for granted and never to discount what our young professionals had to offer.

OPENING THE DOOR TO CONSULTATION - LIMITATIONS

The experience of the Program staff indicated that the most effective way to open doors to consultation was measured and effective service delivery in those instances when the personnel of the other agency lacked and needed the expertise of mental health workers. It was necessary to maximize contact with agencies where there seemed to be the possibility of a fruitful consultation relationship. This meant going out to the agency (not summoning their personnel) whenever possible. Then, avoiding immediate commitments, it was necessary to find out from the people who might be the consultees what services it might be reasonable to offer to them and their clients. Over time it became possible with key individuals to develop a trust and a professional form of friendship, which tended to obviate much of the ritual posturing and defensiveness so often attendant on initial meetings. Enduring and productive relationships could be developed in this fashion, and with care it was possible to build in an assessment of needs.

It was not desirable to make any immediate exaggerated promises during an initial contact, particularly over the telephone. There were usually so many unwritten and hidden agendas that premature promises could lead to a great deal of wasted time and effort. I found there was never, ever a simple open message. Even when the call was only to arrange for a weekly case conference, acceptance had the potential for leading to a premature commitment to something that both sides might wish they had not embarked upon.

For example, if a school called about discussing cases, it was often found that their idea of the proper focus of concern was a truant child who their personnel did not want to handle. Or a child presented for referral might require a physical examination which might be available at the school. Rather than pursue this line of work themselves, they wished to have the consultant (who was no longer a consultant but becoming a deliverer of direct services at the school) do all the information gathering and in the case of a truant child, the consultant might become a punitive arm of the school. In essence the recalcitrant child (or parent) was to be punished by banishment to therapy. Naturally, it was a rather touchy situation, when there was no apparent psychopathology, to attempt to enter a home noting only the "symptom" of truancy. There may well have been considerable pathology, but the child may also have been responding logically to a school situation from which he could not benefit or where he felt threatened.

Initial contacts might lead to "dumping" or referring cases that had not been evaluated properly. Dumping was common when readily accessible information was not made available to the person in the other agency receiving the referral, where the person in the other agency did not want to do the possibly uninteresting or regrettable work involved, and the case might in reality be hopeless or inappropriate. Sometimes, in hopes of gaining entry into an important system such as a welfare department or a school, there was the inclination to overlook the dictates of better judgment and accede to the demands, but inevitably there was a withdrawal when the nature of the inappropriate task was realized. This later withdrawal created more ill will than standing firm on appropriate guidelines at the beginning and possibly working out a reasonable and realistic agreement. Even if an initial refusal closed the door on a system or its subsystem, when no other action was possible, there was, in the long run, little lost. There was often a way to keep the door ajar, but there were frequent points when demands were so inappropriate, that it had to be firmly closed.

If an acceptable agreement could be worked out, the staff found it reasonable to request the consultees to assemble information most available to them and to carry out activities within their purview. In the instances when the conference resulted in a distinct case referral, they were logically asked to prepare the individual for the arrival of mental health personnel and most preferably to introduce the worker. When these basic matters were not attended to, unsuspecting staff members were confronted by a person who did not know them, did not know they were coming, and did not want to see them.

In doing this early work to build the relationship and accept cases, it was always desirable to develop a method for regular meetings at the facility of the consultee rather than accepting referrals over the telephone with a promise of relevant information to come. The primary purpose in the face-to-face contact was to pursue the building of a worthwhile relationship, personally as well as professionally.

If the relationship was developed carefully on the basis of shared problems and the willingness of the mental health personnel to accept appropriate cases, then a reasonable footing was gained. It was necessary to view appropriate service as the essential first step. This meant being firm on what could and could not be done and not accepting the dumping of inappropriate cases which were either well beyond the type of help agreed upon or had not been considered for alternative handling

- where the personnel of the other agency had not done the requisite research on the case or explored referrals to other agencies.

If the agency personnel could accept the necessary limitations, then there was the possibility for genuine discussion of cases that could lead much further. We could avoid wasting time delivering services in cases that the other agency hadn't properly assessed. We could know what had already been done on the case and so avoid duplication of effort. Then too, when the information at their command was assessed, it might be possible to make a mutual assessment of a more appropriate course of action. It could be seen that consultation in principle, had already begun when there was a worthwhile exchange of case information in a discussion format.

Having avoided initial problems, it was possible to begin working with some individuals at the other agency, and when they understood our willingness to give realistic help, then more people became interested and more widely productive meetings could be arranged. It was even desirable to bend a little in the information gathering, when it was clear that, at least for the moment, they needed help doing it.

The realities of the setting indicated that the primary operating principle was opportunism. It was pointless to sit in a smoke-filled room and decide on target agencies when there was no knowledge of how open they were to a relationship. Not all schools are alike and not all sections of large urban agencies are alike. An innocent telephone call from one individual at a crucial moment might be just the opportunity necessary to open many doors and eventually lead to worthwhile cooperation.

If there was haste to maintain an impressive list of consultation activities, there might be a tendency to retain an agency as a recipient of services too long or to take on too much too soon. Agencies rise and fall, centralize and decentralize, and changes in State and Federal Government policies can cripple an agency's effectiveness overnight. Even the most magnificent consultant may be unable to benefit them. At the same time another agency may be blossoming under new leadership and, if service lures had been offered at opportune moments and if clues were attended to and reasonable groundwork laid, a new, vigorous relationship might be developed..

Throughout, it was important to keep in mind what another could and could not do. For example, if a child needed a psychological evaluation, it might be available through the school – in six months to a year. In cases of crisis, the best way to make a positive input to foster future developments and meet a genuine need was to accept such a case while resisting acceptance of evaluations that were not necessarily crucial or could clearly wait. Otherwise, the consulting agency might become a service arm of the school system and not a needed independent resource that could respond in emergencies. Of course, after reviewing the case, the consultant was to accept the evaluation responsibility only when he agreed that it was necessary.

There was a tendency to overestimate, at early stages of a case, what a given system might be able to do. Most agencies had serious limitations in their ability to serve their clients either through financial assistance and ancillary services, in the case of the welfare system, or in evaluation and training in salable skills in training programs for the poor, for example. By recognizing limitations and by accepting appropriate referrals while providing needed assistance, agencies could develop a relationship that would make agency personnel more interested in developing preventive skills or methods of operation. Such a development might include the consultee's ability to do more on all aspects of a case themselves. The delicate balance was found in providing sufficient time to develop a relationship that could be productive in future consultation and accepting just enough cases to be of assistance but not overburdening the mental health agency to the extent that it had no time for appropriate consultation.

It was entirely possible that the phase of opening the door could take at least months and possibly years, although it was hardly productive to spend years playing games with agency personnel who give clear signals they wanted no part of the consultant but would not say so directly. Even when the head of the agency was unsympathetic to goals beyond case referral, friends were being made at lower levels who could be invaluable when the winds shifted within the agency.

At the beginning, the glad hand extended by an agency representative had to be suspect. Any agency person greeting a person presenting himself as a consultant has a right to make his own assessment of the potential consultant, and caution is indicated on their parts as well as on the part of the consultant. What may seem to be a magnificent opening to a prized, productive consultation relationship too frequently turned to ashes. Thus, there had to be the willingness to enter extended negotiations and build a relationship on the basis of honest and appropriate help.

Ideally, in the early stages of a relationship, realistic information on the true functioning of the agency had been gathered while cases were being accepted, emergencies handled, and meetings held. Such a time was a perfect opportunity to increase the depth of understanding of the functioning of the agency. While posturing was occurring in meetings and some modest socializing took place, information was being gathered on agency problems. The mental health worker could, during this time period, assess personality problems of agency personnel, counterproductive agency policies, internal agency politics, external politics affecting the agency, and who really wields power and the nature of their territory. All of this information was extremely useful when the opportunity presented itself for systems change. Above all, there had to be a reasonable view that information gathering was not Machiavellian in intent but rather an honest assessment of how the consultant as a (hoped for) objective outsider with a useful form of expertise might help the personnel of the agency do more and become more effective.

Organizational charts told next to nothing about who was really running the agency and perhaps told little more than who was paid the most. It was desirable to ascertain wherein the real power resides. There might be a person in a high-level position who did not really have power in terms of day-to-day functioning but must not be overlooked or at least must be apprised of progress. This continued to be a factor even when consultation was well established.

Likewise, the consultant had to continue to be aware of what the program was really doing. Not infrequently the program narrative or grant proposal bore little relationship to how the program really functioned. What was written on paper usually hid a large number of issues and the consultant had to continue to develop a working knowledge of the agency. If systems change was sought on the basis of written material, then the work might be an utter failure because it would not relate to the hard facts of reality.

As noted in the section on goals, weekly meetings were not necessarily a success in terms of making real changes even when the highest-level personnel were engaged. Without a working knowledge of the agency, the wrong people might be included in the meeting and the consultant was prevented from talking with those individuals who could make policy statements and organizational change truly effective. A rationale for including these people, even though the organizational chart did not dictate their inclusion, could often be found.

Just as there had to be a continuing assessment of their functioning, the consultant continued to assess his own functioning at every step. The goal was to help them and not help oneself except in the sense of learning. Although the consultant could become happy with what he was doing, the effects may only be short term and he might fail utterly in assisting them with long term problems. The relationship and the work of the consultation must be considered to be at least potentially in flux. The consultant must be prepared to shift emphasis and be just as opportunistic in the developed consulting relationship as he was in taking or making opportunities to develop a relationship. It was necessary to remember the reasons for being there—to help improve their functioning and service delivery through sharing useful elements of the mental health body of knowledge and methods.

The needs of each agency were sufficiently different that presenting these general points is more useful than for me to go into particulars of the work with a given agency. Only through the detailed assessment of their functioning and problems at the beginning could the consultant make his individual assessment of the exact form of intervention. This was where the independence and the skill of the consultant came into play. This skill included picking up on intuitive notions of appropriate activities and noting when the direction chosen is going badly or well and why.

A consulting relationship should not be looked at as fixed and continuing indefinitely. Just as with a client or patient when assistance may be suspended for indefinite periods either for purposes of consolidation or because immediate problems have been solved, the consultant must be prepared to suspend consultation work. There may be unavoidable changes within an agency that make advisable an interruption in the relationship. In order not to be forgotten in the rush of other business, we usually tried to retain some ties or find excuses to meet with agency personnel periodically. But if the relationship was to truly endure, the consultant must know when to leave. He must also be aware that there are times when he sees failure in his efforts because, perhaps, he was not able to promote an identified need for staff training along the lines of his own desires. However, he may have often done just as much or more if he had facilitated change in some key policies. A simple change may have startling immediate effects or promote slow steady changes.

The key elements in a successful relationship, then, revolved around recognition of limitations, slow change, careful development of a relationship based on meaningful assistance, and clear recognition of when to step out. A consultant could not afford the luxury of concentrating on the short-term view of the activity. Rather, he had to be continuously aware of the more subtle long-range movements and maintain a perspective on a larger time scale.

There are two very different waves of change and movement in an agency. It can be affected by day-to-day factors, but there is a much slower form of wave that is probably more important. Being aware of this may be the most important contribution an objective outsider can make.

The political environment and, in the inner city, the effects of national politics were so important that they may well determine much of the success of a consultation relationship. When the Program began operation in Baltimore, the inner city was alive and vital, with growing social action or helping programs. Many of these programs were in the first thrust of their endeavors, and frequently their staffs were extremely enthusiastic. They wanted to learn and were open to outside consultation except in the case of agencies whose staff felt they had the "world by the tail" and could solve all the problems themselves.

Within a year after the Nixon administration came into office, the inner city was again showing signs of being a wasteland, with increasingly depressed and apathetic staff members in the publicly financed programs. It was clear already that at best the new administration was uninterested or at worst was hostile to their endeavors. Money was being cut from budgets; the policy guidelines were beginning to change and indicated a more punitive orientation toward the poor. New guidelines tended toward policies contrary to what the staffs had learned would be effective. Matters grew considerably and consistently worse.

Although there might be considerable work that a consultant could do in theory, in actuality the collective depression that was gathering inhibited all work except in carefully selected situations. Thus, it was necessary to make even more careful choices about recipients of consultation because many administrators were reaching for anything that might lift the morale of their staffs while they wrestled with their deep sense of betrayal. The probability of success was slim, particularly in cases where federal policy guidelines were key issues. Even a modern messiah couldn't have turned around some of these staffs and prevented the loss of some of the best people. Whereas there had been a feast at the beginning and there had to be judicious choices because of limited resources, continuing deterioration in the helping agencies indicated the need for even more judicious choices because of the deterioration of the situation.

SUMMARY

Implicit in the statement of goals outlined in this chapter is the assumption that there are more ways for consultation to go wrong than there are ways for it to go right. Nonetheless, it is, in the end, a desirable endeavor for the reasons stated by Caplan and because the body of knowledge of the community mental health field can benefit other persons and agencies both in the clinical and organizational area.

Unfortunately, too often we saw a grandiosity which led to failure of a consultation. The consultant often seemed to offer the body of mental health knowledge and procedures as a panacea. When lower-level staff arrived to continue the relationship, they could not possibly live up to exaggerated expectations. In addition, the relationship had to operate within a changing and confusing field reflecting class factors, economic policies, and social policies. It was essential to recognize that in opening doors, impatience was wholly inappropriate. Caplan recognized this fact, but it was often forgotten by professionals in the field.

In these past decades, the pace of social change seemed to be constantly increasing, and institutions and the people running them were hard-pressed to adapt to the changing demands. As consultants we not only had to address the seemingly focal issues but also had to realize human limitations and aid, wherever possible, the individuals to make the necessary adaptations. Young staff tended to be impatient, particularly in an era of reform, and had to recognize that as consultants they were part of the "establishment". Revolutionary change was beyond their purview.

From our vantage point of the 1960s, we could see ruinous decline in the cities. What we could not see was that even worse was to come. The crack epidemic had not yet arrived, and the deterioration was to be worse in every way. Yet, we were impatient, and impatience remained an enemy in an ongoing battle. The art of the possible was forever an elusive goal.

From the beginning there was a purist element in community mental health that saw the only proper role of the mental health professional as that of an agent of systems change and primary prevention. The ideal was the pure consultant who did not waste his time on cases and supported an almost mystical view of primary prevention. The most cynical view of this position I heard was that, in the inner city, primary prevention was designed primarily to prevent professionals from coming face-to-face with poor people.

Mental health is merely a cog in the machine of change, and that change is shaped by a much larger fund of forces. In the inner city, we found our beginning in direct service, with consultation only possible after an arduous building of relationships based on a strong reality focus. The casualties had to be attended to first, and then consultation relationships could be sought.

The arguments for a primary prevention consultation focus are compelling on paper but take on a different reality in the inner city. Failure to give service and relate to the community needs as a whole may cost mental health workers influence and lead to charges of imperialism. The rate of change brought about by consultation, even when the most damaging errors were avoided, was so excruciatingly slow that workers faced the loss of popular support, broad-based assistance and cooperation.

Whatever Happened to Community Mental Health?

Of all services expected to be offered by a community mental health center, consultation is by far the most glamorous. Or at least reading the literature suggested it was glamorous, and typically successes got into print rather than much needed "how to do it" material. The classic book Closed Ranks by Cumming and Cumming is perhaps an outstanding exception, in view of the fact that they honestly assess how difficult it is to measure success and impact in changing attitudes. Their book signaled a welcome shift in emphasis toward realistic assessments just when the bloom was leaving the community mental health rose and the people involved in the movement had to face themselves.

In the very beginning of the community mental health movement, much of the consultation received by the staff was directed at theory and how they in turn could give consultation. Problem-solving laboratories keyed to working on specific issues would have been much more appropriate. Such workshops would have required extensive ground work being laid by both the consultant and the recipient of consultation.

Given the newness of the enterprise in the inner city, consultants would have done better to come in and assess what we were really seeing and how the community operated. Instead the presentations conveyed an assumption that the consultant had come with answers, whereas the procedures offered often were contrary to what our experience was showing us. In fact, we needed to voice the reality of our experiences with agencies and community organizations and look together at how the consultation relationship might be improved. As a staff we did that very thing informally, and an open relationship with some of the consultants would have enhanced the process. But too often it seemed we were assumed to be ignorant. Just as some therapists believed they were in a never-ending process of learning from their patients, the mental health consultant should have been in a never-ending posture of learning from the people with whom he consulted.

Consultation can be very exciting and moves the mental health worker from the mystery story of the one-to-one relationship of psychotherapy to the mystery story of systems operation and change. In both cases there may be dynamic short-term occurrences, but there is also a long-term movement, slower and more difficult to perceive. However, the view of the consultant must also extend beyond the recipient agency when issues of state or national policy operate; under attack from inimical outside forces, the consultant may assume the armor, trappings and functioning of Don Quixote.

The attention that Gerald Caplan and other proponents have paid to preventive consultation based on the public health models was appropriate in that it pointed out larger variables that affect the mental health of whole populations. These variables and policies still deserve attention but, despite the model's excellent impression on paper, it does not, in fact, work very well in practice. Most agencies want help, not advice, and because they are generally overwhelmed with the problems of the people they serve, their own organizational problems, and often their personal problems, they do not listen. The professional who is determined to make the Caplan model work under such circumstances is quite likely to engage in self-delusion about productivity and fall prey to elitism and self-protection. With a balanced perspective and dedication to direct service and personal involvement where it is appropriate and needed, people in the mental health field in the inner city can give desirable and qualitative services and then, when there is an opportunity to affect larger issues, they can be in a firm reality position to make the most of them.

Chapter 4
Functions and Problems of Professionals

CONTEXT

Working in a community mental health program, especially in an inner city setting was a new, if not unique, experience at the time. Some of the issues the staff had to deal with personally were common to other settings and some were not. The reader should have little difficulty, however, in relating the basic problems to other settings where professionals must relate to people substantially different from themselves.

The issues noted in this chapter reflect observations of problems seen in the Program and the staff. These problems affected service and organizational matters.

CHOOSING THE JOB

Choosing community mental health work in an almost universally impoverished inner city setting meant plain and simple hard work. We had to question why any sane professional would seek a job in such a setting. Naturally, the dark humor of the staff tended to focus on questioning our sanity for taking such a job. One view was that the romantic notion of serving the "noble poor" constituted a danger to the maintenance of our own optimal and realistic functioning.

Early on I also had to question my own motives for choosing this job. The fact of the matter was that I really did not like school but endured it all the way through getting a Ph.D. Also, after all those years in academia I was ready for a change.

My appetite for change and alternatives had been whetted by a small program Duke had run bringing evaluations of school children to a poor tidewater county in North Carolina. The evaluations permitted the school system to document need and to get much needed federal funds. The description of this poor rural county portrayed its major resources as sand and gravel. It was ruled like a barony by a small group of White families. Lunch for the Black children was generally at a small local store where they bought a soda and a desert cake. The experience left me motivated to get involved in the process of change.

At the time the civil rights movement was quite active. Civil rights workers had been murdered in Mississippi. There were marches in the streets of Durham. Once, dinner in a local restaurant involved sitting next to a group of policemen loudly proclaiming what they were going to do to the expletives deleted.

These experiences contrasted with my life as a young child in a privileged family. There were times when the commuter train going to Grand Central Station would stop in Harlem. My face would be glued to the window as I looked down 125th. Street or into apartments. I asked my mother who these people were and why they were living the way they did. She did not have good answers. In the end I think I had to find out about it for myself many years later.

It seemed that all staff members had their own special reasons for being there. It was more than a job.

ADJUSTMENT OF STAFF MEMBERS

Regardless of the motivation for coming to work in the Program, staff had a virtually inevitable personal crisis during the first six months or year. It was a personal crisis wherein they felt worthless and believed that they did not possess sufficient therapeutic skills to "heal" their clients. No discussion of this eventuality seemed to prevent it.

Even when the clinicians had had considerable previous therapy experience, they came to feel that somehow they should be able to do more and be able to help more of their clients, and that the root of the client's problem was the clinician's own professional, if not personal, inadequacy. As the casualties continued to crowd in the door, the responsible senior professionals and experienced staff in general had to be prepared to give emotional support to the staff members in crisis while they made the crucial adjustment to accept what was reasonably possible.

The appropriate resolution of the crisis yielded a more mature worker who knew when to give up, alter approaches, and accept inevitable defeats even in what might have been a promising case. If they failed to make this adjustment, they became anxious, eventually depressed, and finally hostile or apathetic toward their clients.

When the hostility appeared, if it was generally not displaced to other staff members, it might be turned on the clients with the resolution that they must be "bad", "no good", "slackers", and generally deserving of their fate.

The staff who fell to this position came to it from a defensive posture related to threat regarding self esteem. (They had little in common with some "conservatives" of today who seem to hold others who are less fortunate in contempt and use comparison to elevate their own self worth.) Typically, with support from experienced staff, they would resolve the problem or they would move on.

No matter what, it seemed, given the extreme distress found among inner city residents, that any professional's time in a "line" position was limited. Even a well-adjusted individual facing the same endless stream of casualties must sooner or later become jaded and apathetic or must design an exit strategy. Even with appropriate resolution of the typical crises, it appeared that each person must sooner or later leave, if only for a change of pace or setting.

Crises could take other forms. One morning, shortly after I arrived at work, another staff member came to me to report that one of our staff had not shown up for work. She was an extremely reliable person and, for reasons we could not entirely fathom, we were alarmed. A call to her apartment yielded no answer. We went to her apartment and knocked. No response.

After a while we found a maintenance man and took responsibility for him to unlock the door to her apartment, but the chain was on. We could hear labored breathing inside. I tried my shoulder against the door and just bounced off. The maintenance man palmed it sharply and the door tore open.

We found her near death from a prescription drug overdose and got her to the hospital in time to save her life. All we could know was that one of our own was missing and we found her in distress. How much of her distress was a personal matter and how much the job contributed we would never know. We also didn't know what alarmed us in this instance, but we did watch out for each other and knew where each person was in order to provide a measure of safety in a difficult physical and personal environment.

Over time, among the staff, we saw instances of heroin addiction and alcohol abuse. All of these issues were mixed in with the types of problems we saw in staff members burning out or in many ways reaching the limits of their time with this type of job.

STAFF ROMANTICISM

It seemed in those days that romanticism was everywhere and the management of it was crucial to the success of the Program. The downtrodden were to be served and the endeavors were noble as well intentioned professionals strove to heal the wounds inflicted by racism and life in an economically disadvantaged position.

In the inner city setting we encountered an endless flow of what the staff of the Program frequently referred to as "casualties". They were to be served in the best possible fashion, which meant that the realities of their existence had to be carefully assessed and intervention made with care and speed. When a staff member became overidentified with a client and his problems, he could spend endless hours in fruitless efforts to solve problems with no solutions. Even worse, he might spend hours on a case with such hardened pathology that little if any change was possible.

We had to learn about romance; we found that romantic clinicians were prone to therapeutic errors and joked that they might actually turn an acute crisis into a chronic problem. In time both the patient and the staff member might become chronic cases. The staff member could eventually be diagnosed as a chronic case of the "bleeding heart syndrome". In this syndrome the clinician sought out the most horrifying and impossible cases on which to dwell and ignored the art of the possible. We envisioned a never-ending quixotic charge as he sought to remedy the world's ills through intervention with a few pathetic individuals who deserved some but not all of a professional's attention. It was interesting to see that these romantics-gone-wrong were sometimes capable of mobilizing the energies of major agencies by finding similarly oriented staff members in each.

Many times the romantic seeking to help the poor labored with the misperception that those poor must be Black. As noted already, Black people were not the exclusive inhabitants of the inner city, and the existence of this kind of romanticism meant there was the potential for getting off to a bad start by overlooking the existence of the White population.

Romanticism might also involve unrealistic expectations of magnificent changes and a tendency to believe too much in the effectiveness of the mental health body of knowledge. A simplistic view suggested that when persons who have been deprived and denied opportunity, were offered the denied chance, the individual's perspective on life would be altered, he would embrace the opportunity, and it would permit him to overcome his environment. Rationally, most professionals knew better.. Expectations do not magically change, tools are needed and attitudes must change. There are so many impediments.

Thus, the romantic nature and general motivation of potential staff members had always to be examined; for they might either be totally unable to function in the light of reality or might need guidance until they gained perspective. Unless the romanticism was handled appropriately and realistically, the staff person would either remain in the "bleeding heart" cul-de-sac or inevitable disillusionment would occur with attendant anger and eventual apathy. The morale of the entire unit could be endangered by a debilitating apathy that would spread to other adequately functioning staff members.

GUILTY LIBERALS

When a reasonable concern for the well-being of the poor became a never-ending quest to assuage a personal feeling of guilt, the clinician could be described as a "guilty liberal" who had become dysfunctional. In one extreme form the liberal (probably White) might seek punishment from Black militants in the community. An ideal way to achieve this end would be to seek and receive an assignment to develop an advisory board of indigenous persons.

Forgive the seeming cynicism, but it was an ongoing concern that some staff might bow to the wishes of the most vocal militants. The individual in question would typically be well-intentioned but could lead the program into a major crisis. If a board was formed with dysfunctional or self-serving persons, it might have to be disbanded under difficult circumstances.

It was not exclusively a White problem; we saw it in Black professionals who nursed their own kind of guilt. In some cases they might feel considerable guilt about their own professional and financial success and might return to serve their less fortunate people. The goal may be appropriate and laudatory, but they could become dysfunctional.

Staff members had to be alert to these themes in themselves, and examination, even if only privately, was encouraged. The attributes of romanticism, a crisis in belief in oneself, and some guilt might all be present, but in moderation they constituted reasonable motives for taking the job or finding ways to learn. The balance of effectiveness often depended upon the degree of mastery, and type of resolution.

RACISM AND RACE

In the liberal professional environment, overt manifestations of racism and prejudice were so severely frowned upon that they were quickly lost from a person's response system or forced, unexamined, underground. When there was no resolution or reasonable control of prejudice, it simply changed form and was seen in the more pervasive forms of fawning insincerity and deferential treatment, sometimes through the vehicle of promotions. This form of racism was much more difficult to confront and was just as effective as the more blatant form of prejudice in galling and demeaning staff members. It was even more dangerous because it could be so subtle that the victim might not be aware of the reason for his discomfort, and even when he was aware, it could be nearly impossible to effectively deal with it or confront it.

Differential and deferential treatment of Black staff members had the effect of devaluing them as people. They came to wonder for what reason they were hired or promoted. Such doubts could in no way foster effective functioning or feelings of self-worth.

This type of racism caused White administrators to be blinded to the diversity that existed among Black professionals. To vastly oversimplify the situation for purposes of illustration, it was possible to define three groups: outspoken militants, "Uncle Toms", and professionals who simply wished to perform a good job and might be apolitical. Racist liberals tended to hire the first type, rejected the second type, and saw the third type as being part of the second. The prejudice, guilt, and potential for resentment and dysfunction was obvious.

The program staff experienced one serious incident when some staff assignments were changed on the basis of race alone. The Civil Rights Commission (of Maryland) produced a poorly developed and ill-founded report that accused the Program of racism. Indeed, there was some minor tendency to place staff according to race, but the tendency was generally minor and on occasions represented reverse racism. The imbalance in staff related more to chance in available staff positions and the qualified individuals who arrived at a given moment to fill them. In what approached a panic response, central administrative officials made some reassignments on the basis of race without considering the skills and probable function of the staff members involved. At least one person was transferred from a position in which he was quite effective to one in which he was considerably less so. There was a great deal of staff bitterness at what was viewed as a betrayal.

While trying to be fair in hiring, it was hard to justify a change in assignment because of race alone. Decisions made in the light of this exclusive characteristic had highly deleterious effects on programmatic functioning. Equally, where there had been intended or unintended racism in hiring, attempts to remedy the situation by hiring virtually any Black professional available could lead to a disaster. The new staff member might, for a variety of reasons, be unsuited to the position and become demoralized by the lack of opportunity to develop his or her actual skills.

It is difficult to describe how hard it was to achieve balance on the race issue in those days. To be constantly vigilant sets up an artificial almost totalitarian atmosphere. To attend to it not at all would leave open the possibility of unfortunate errors. Mostly we were able to achieve balance.

We were also tested by outside events, the worst of which was the assassination of Martin Luther King, Jr. We were working in harmony when this cataclysmic event occurred. On the morning after the assassination, we came to work and had to face each other. How could the White staff conceivably know what his death meant to the Black staff? How was the Black staff to view us? Could we again work in harmony?

The answer was that we could and had to. Baltimore was burning around us. We dealt with each other, carefully and touchingly at first. In time we healed our own wounds. The riots grew in intensity, and we had to choose when and how to again go out into the community. Our first step was to start calling our clients to check on their status. It was a revelation to find that they were actually doing better. The riots brought out the need to see to personal safety and a shared concern about the future, which temporarily healed their personal concerns. But it was only temporary.

In retrospect I view the day Dr. King was murdered as one of the most damaging days in our country's history. Looking back I could see the beginning of the disillusion of the working relationship between Blacks and Whites in so many ways. Gradually I could feel that we were less welcome. The hand that had been extended was slowly withdrawn. The bold experiment was ending, at least in part. We had made gains, but it would never quite be the same. And yet work in our society continued until, 40 years later, we made the great stride of electing a Black president.

In those decades, damage continued within the Black community. A split seemed to be developing. The people who were determined to make it up and out continued on their way, and many left to a better position in life. Many other people seemed to fall back into hopelessness and a permanent position among the "left-behinds". I have to admit I did not study the phenomenon, but this is how it felt to me as the years passed. And now suddenly there is renewed opportunity and support for aspirations with the emergence of a Black First Family.

ACTIVIST STAFF – LISTEN!

The staff members of the community mental health program tended to view themselves as change agents. It seemed characteristic of persons attracted to such programs. The role of change agent might include anything from a strong emphasis on change within a system to confrontation with outside agencies.

Within bounds there was clearly a place for activism but its form of it had to be dictated by the political realities of the situation. Activism usually is not described as including the normal, accepted, institutionalized role of the moderate consultant working with other agencies. Activism in this case meant testing the possibilities and limitations of a change orientation directed at the mental health organization itself by its own staff. Such activist persons might not limit their activities to confrontation within a given program.

Changes might be sought within the mental health organization or in the total health system. But there had to be a realization that the staff as a body was in many ways very much a part of the establishment. As such, there were distinct bounds to permissible activism. In achieving some balance of activism, it was necessary to realize that, if services were worthwhile, there was the obligation to continue those services and seek to increase funding.

We had to help activist staff understand that precipitous actions, which exceeded reasonable expectations of the rate of change, might merely serve to generate hostility from higher-ups and actually decrease funding. The end result could be fewer effective services for clients and no real change, while the traditionalist forces hardened their resistance.

If the confrontations reached public form, it was an open admission of the failure of discussion and grievance procedures. Rarely could such public confrontations be considered constructive unless the situation was so totally without merit that almost any change – even loss of services – seemed justified. It was difficult to imagine in what instance it might be justifiable to curtail services while reforms were sought. I refer specifically to interference within the organization, but clearly there might be externally induced confrontations that were beyond our control. In either case, however, confrontation with the community should be unnecessary if the community and its spokesmen were not misperceived.

Some professionals showed a tendency toward grandiosity, in its most inappropriate form appearing to be a claim to omniscience. It was bad enough when such tendencies were inflicted upon professionals in other agencies, but it was even worse when there was a failure to take account of diverse and potentially valid viewpoints within the mental health organization itself. The staff needed to continue to carefully examine the validity of their own positions, and activities and to foster maximum open communications within their immediate ranks.

The staff were attempting to find new paths and were not automatically ready to follow people with status gained by virtue of high rank and education They came to believe that the role of leadership was most properly earned not by job tenure but by worthwhile development of staff potential, efficiency of operation, and delivery of useful services. This is not to say that we abdicated the right to discipline irresponsible staff but rather, that we heard grievances and maintained an open-door policy.

Services for the poor were typically financed by public funds and the staff had to consider themselves to be a part of an "establishment" agency. Therefore, responsible staff were often discouraged from activist maneuvering within the mental health system and were encouraged to direct their work in areas open to them on their own time.

But there was an activism allied with independence. We, as junior staff, had a curious viewpoint. We did not automatically assume that we would accept the senior staff as being people who possessed wisdom. We were engaged in a new kind of activity in a difficult setting. We came to believe that higher-level staff had to earn the right to lead by proving themselves. Such a viewpoint on the part of junior staff may sound outlandish, but looking back with the wisdom of another forty years experience, I still believe it was a valid viewpoint.

In the Program many of our "superiors" flunked miserably. They had to be willing to listen to lower-status and younger staff who frequently had well thought-out positions and viewpoints based on their closer relationship to the delivery of direct service and consultation with outside agencies.

In return the junior staff had their own obligation to be responsible in their demands. The farther the administrative leadership was removed from the problems of delivering the services, the greater was the possibility that they might no longer be accounting for variables that had only recently come into the purview of the organization. And, of course, then there were the previously described differences in values and agenda. The individuals in leadership positions could prove themselves by maintaining a desire to continue learning and to maximize contacts that would permit them to view the problems of their service delivery staff. Thus, methods for hearing the basic experiences of the staff and their ideas were imperative, and a willingness to weigh with them their ideas and experiences could have obviated the need for activism within the organization.

For us, activism within the organization became essential. Grandiose directors were often attracted to these kinds of programs. In moderation some grandiosity might be useful, but at times the grandiosity went beyond all reasonable bounds.

The program seemed valued mostly for the funds it yielded rather than as an endeavor worth studying and developing. Our Program was foreign to the University and the State did not value it and what might be learned from it. Oversight was one from lofty positions far away. And then we were suddenly saddled with a director who verged on the bizarre. He grandly declared that we should break all bounds of clinical service. He insisted we had to be truly open to the community, which meant our sessions with our clients would be held in large rooms open to all comers. In addition, the director wished us to stage "peaking events" for the community, which were ill-defined but seemed carnival-like events of celebration to bring all people together and heal all wounds.

When the staff objected and wished to be heard, the response of the director was to threaten staff with demotion or dismissal even as he continued to declare that he had the solution to the problems of the cities of America. Messiah-like outbursts occurred in meetings with other community agencies. Staff anger was rising and morale crumbling.

On December 9, 1968 what became known as the "Palace Rebellion" occurred as a number of us tried to sit down with the director and express our viewpoints. The meeting deteriorated into angry outbursts and threats by the director. There followed a number of tumultuous full staff meetings.

The staff saw our consultation relationships being destroyed and our carefully nurtured climate of trust with our clients and the community dissolving. We resisted ever more vehemently and he, in turn, demanded absolute loyalty, which he did not get. Carl, our lead community organizer, wrote up a detailed "indictment" of the director indicating he was clearly willing to put his own career on the line. It was virtually nailed to the door of the Director of the Psychiatric Institute. Several of us joined him in the meeting that followed. We met with a completely bewildered, elderly psychiatrist who had obviously never seen such an outrageous uprising by young professionals. In a quiet, determined and reasonable fashion the problems and excesses were documented.

The turmoil continued and resistance hardened while events moved slowly. Then came the headline in the *Baltimore Sun* on February 19, 1969. "U.M. Demotes Director of Ghetto Mental Program". Shortly the director resigned; and the staff of the "mental program" had prevailed.

ACTIVIST STAFF – CONTROL!

Although the staff had expected to have channels for continuous, judicious change within the range of what would be responsible with public funding and the political climate, there had also to be, on the part of the leadership, a willingness to exercise control. At times it had to be unpleasant control over individuals who took money for being "professional" but divided the staff and the program from the community. The consequences of control, even if it had to be reasonably public and painful, were generally miniscule compared to the mistrust and conflict which could be generated within a program and between the community and the program if left unchecked. Such situations invariably would deteriorate until action was finally taken. Disruptions of some programs around the country at the time indicated that this type of problem existed in many settings.

Sometimes activism was related to very personal agendas. When a troublesome individual or group expressed an interest in the well-being of the members of the community, it in no way ruled out deep-rooted prejudice against the people supposedly being championing. We saw professionals and people within the community who were interested only in their personal aggrandizement and power. In one such person on the staff we saw an amazing transformation. He was a perennial activist, but later he moved up high into the mental health system and transformed himself into the consummate bureaucrat. The transformation spoke volumes about his real motives.

We came to see that unbounded and unrestrained activism or militancy might represent genuine psychopathology. There seemed to be militants who behaved neurotically and unconsciously had no desire to achieve their stated goals. Rather, they set about their activities in such a fashion that there was no reasonable chance of achieving their goals and they would only further increase the destructive influences of a relatively unresponsive system.

At times we saw professional staff members ally themselves with some militants in the community to validate their shared negative expectations of the world. The particular agency or program attacked was unimportant so long as they created a crisis and failed utterly in bringing about any worthwhile changes. When they walked out in disgust after having endangered functioning, inhibited services, and immobilizing an agency for a period, they had achieved their goal of proving to themselves the essential malevolence of the world and all those who hold power. They could then, with angry satisfaction, nurse their wounds, commiserate, and seek a new target.

We were generally alert to such activities. If real attempts to solve real problems revealed no motivation to reach a reasonable solution, then painful controls had to be exercised. There was no way to "win" in such a situation but intervention at the earliest stages was infinitely less damaging than permitting time for the crisis to blossom. Unfortunately, professionals often hoped the problem would go away because they still believed in gentlemen who settled their problems subtly and within carefully defined negotiation sessions. Such luxuries were rarely possible. The situation required a willingness to meet challenges early and recognize that an inner city setting neither spawned nor attracted "gentlemen".

Once I and the lead community organizer spotted a relatively new staffer who was not forming good alliances either within the staff or the community. We became convinced that his functioning would prove highly deleterious. Removing a staff member from a state system was difficult, but we finally prevailed, much against the inclinations of the director. Three months later the man was arrested for arson.

PSYCHIATRISTS

Thus far the discussion in this chapter has related to general staff problems. Let us now discuss the four major professions in turn.

Traditionally psychiatrists have held and still possess the key powers in a mental health organization. At the time their training was still largely focused on individual therapy tending to be strongly oriented to Freud's theories. The focus did not conform well to new modalities of functioning needed in treating the poor. Unfortunately, their training seemed to militate against the consideration of social and cultural factors in generating "mental illness". There were leaders such as Caplan with a broader scope, but such was not our typical psychiatrist. A recognition of such things as situational variables emerged only gradually.

Some psychiatrists seemed to fear changing the structure of service delivery systems. Yet, many of them were leaders and important change agents. To some degree their concerns over giving up some of their prerogatives were legitimate, but we had a serious manpower shortage and their roles had to change in order to meet that need. Other needed changes would have led to many new groups of paraprofessionals taking on much of the direct service delivery and improving the effectiveness of the delivery of services, and it would have had the interesting effect of actually increasing the psychiatrists' impact, status, and income.

Mental health treatment was broadening beyond individual therapy and prescribing medication. The training of psychiatrists was being expanded to require knowledge of resource usage, systems analysis, knowledge of the disciplines of sociology and cultural anthropology and class perspectives. Being conversant with these areas and disciplines appeared crucial if psychiatrists were to move to the necessary roles of planning and management in settings where realities dictated a more central role for the other professions and paraprofessionals in the delivery of direct services.

PSYCHOLOGISTS

Psychologists were heir to some of the same problems as psychiatrists but had a unique problem in their struggle to gain what they saw as equality with psychiatry. With different backgrounds of professional development equality was an uncertain goal at best. Certainly psychologists could legitimately function with considerable autonomy while participating in shaping the changes in the mental health field; psychologists possess independently viable professional skills. By virtue of their training, psychologists possess an eclectic orientation that can foster needed change. Aside from pockets of in-groups that advocate exclusive therapeutic systems, psychologists did broad work in numerous theoretical frameworks. And it is significant that psychology is not the study of pathology but the study of human behavior in general.

Interestingly enough, I found that my research training was particularly valuable in a clinical setting in the inner city, even though I performed no research. The training in itself had yielded a critical faculty that served me well in analyzing the problems with which the Program was faced. While at the time some psychologists were advocating that clinical and experimental psychology become clearly separate entities in training, I found the two types of training to yield singular benefits in multidisciplinary settings when the psychologist was not confined to testing and research – and the Program was not that strictly clinical in any event.

SOCIAL WORKERS

The social work profession attracted individuals who seemed best prepared of all the disciplines to function in an inner city setting. Certainly their training had a major effect on the design of our services, but their success could not be ascribed alone to training and probably related in part to the personalities of the individuals who tended to choose this field of study. Not only were they willing to pitch in and get their hands dirty, but they were also excellent in developing relationships and dealing in a no-nonsense, realistic fashion with outside agencies. Although some might not have had detailed clinical training, they more than made up for it by quickly adapting to a new setting and learning. They came relatively unburdened with rigid ideologies.

In addition, their uniquely useful perspective made it imperative for us to listen to them as we developed services. It was often a humbling experience and added an important dimension to professional development for all the disciplines. There is no need to go on at length. Social workers were the key personnel in mental health in an inner city setting.

PSYCHIATRIC NURSES

Of all the mental health professionals, nurses appeared to be suffering through the worse identity crisis. The nurses in the Program were characteristically able and talented but were very much enmeshed in the nursing dilemma. Nurses had tended to be handmaidens to the physicians, but for an increasing number of women this was no longer a satisfactory role. Many nurses appeared to have entered their profession with traditional sex role expectations. However, with the movement to free women from traditional roles and exploitation, some nurses found themselves uncomfortable with the increasingly unacceptable handmaiden role. The trend was in evidence before large-scale public awareness of the women's liberation movement and certainly typified the dissatisfaction that led to the movement.

It would seem that in the quickly changing field of community mental health, nurses had to do the most soul-searching in identifying a role with which they could become comfortable. With their strong medical background they clearly had a part in the multidisciplinary community mental health organization, but had to come to terms with themselves before they could comfortably adopt a position.

NEW ROLES IN A NEW SETTING

Comments in regard to each of the major traditional professions have been brief because I simply wished to give my view of them and highlight some strengths and weaknesses as we saw them at the time. They are adequately documented elsewhere, from various viewpoints.

The main point is that, as the concept of mental health delivery of services changed, it forced a reexamination of the roles of the traditional professions. Not all professionals can become generalists, and clearly it is impossible to acquire the body of knowledge of all potentially useful disciplines. It is, however, possible for the professions to evaluate the applicability of their skills and utilize them in a multidisciplinary approach to induce growth in each other – the whole being more than the sum of its parts. It seems desirable to build in the flexibility to permit lateral movement to new areas of functioning when an individual is capable, but there will always have to be specialization as circumstances dictate and individuals desire. It was clearly in the future before a new plateau could be reached in defining the respective roles of the disciplines but community mental health in its early years afforded the freedom and opportunity to experiment. While administrators and staff alike sought to solve their collective problems, the individual disciplines wrestled with their problems in working in a reform movement that demanded new functions and new ways of relating to each other. And now we must ask, "How did we do?"

Chapter 5
Administrative and
Organizational Issues

CONTEXT

What did I know about organizations? I had been a graduate student at a major university and my opinion had rarely been asked. But I had been an observer and things were not always as they seemed. And I had a brilliant professor who shared with me his observations about relationships within an organization. He said, "If you see a problem in an organization, don't try to solve the problem. Make it worse so THEY will have to do something about it." I have found those words to live by. Additionally, coming into an organization with which I was not familiar I found another aphorism to be especially important. "Shut up and listen!" And so I watched, listened and learned.

At the time when I was working in Baltimore, mental health organizations were commonly administered by clinically trained professionals. Trained administrators dealt with fiscal matters rather than with the organizational problems and matters of policy necessary to run a mental health program. But, especially in this type of setting, there was a huge gap between the views of administrators of all kinds and young, activist staff.

By administration I will be referring in this chapter to the most senior professionals who were responsible for the clinical and organizational management of the Program. I will not relate to issues such as purchasing and management of funds for program purposes but rather to some of the key functions served by professionals who hired and managed staff while developing and planning for the Program.

The words "filthy lucre" come to mind regarding attitudes about finance and management. At the time no mental health profession prepared its clinically oriented students for an administrative role, even though it was virtually inevitable that they would sooner or later acquire some administrative function. Necessary skills were acquired on the job, and the wild variations in effectiveness of programs run by mental health professionals attested to their varying abilities to acquire and employ the requisite skills.

In the case of the federally originated staffing grant for the community mental health program, there were the five basic services required by law. It was assumed that the provision of such services would be effective, efficient, and as economic as possible. The issue of effectiveness included the most overlooked issue of all – creating an environment in which the staff members would have the opportunity for continuing growth and development. There was more to it than demanding that junior professionals perform duties consistent with the job descriptions. It included making it possible for them to be able to do the job.

When I assumed the position as director of my outpatient unit, I found that my most challenging job was not the management of my staff or services but making it possible for them to do their jobs in spite of the absurdities and interference from the central office, the University, and the State.

Central administration was detached from the staff and knew very little about what we did and did not do on a day-to-day basis. It sounds absurd, but both the University and the State were that detached.

STAFF MANAGEMENT

New staff members faced a problem with which administrators needed to be prepared to help. Staff often found that the roles they saw for themselves were blurred by functional demands. There existed the possibility of a crisis of identity. That is, since so many people were performing similar functions, it became unclear what contribution was unique to a given profession. Assuming the mental health organization was not strictly traditional in its operation, the administrators of the program had to be aware of this crisis and had to be prepared to define jobs clearly for those who required such structure. Where it was not possible to clearly delineate functions relating to professional training, the staff was assisted in recognizing how their own growth and program effectiveness was enhanced by the pooling of their respective bodies of knowledge.

This issue seemed to be a simple one but was frequently overlooked. We had a lovely young woman on our staff who had an instantaneous calming influence on people. All we had to do was send her into a room and the combatants, particularly males, were completely disarmed. Sometimes authority worked, sometimes she was the weapon of choice.

We moved from a vertical hierarchy to a horizontal arrangement with shared responsibilities. In this fashion we avoided the placement of the wrong person in the wrong job by virtue of the possession of a degree.

Sharing responsibility and pooling abilities did not necessarily create a team structure. Creating teams can serve to prevent the breakup of the traditional status hierarchy diffuse responsibility and blame for programs gone awry, as well as wasting monumental amounts of staff and client time. When improperly utilized, teams generate paperwork, meetings, and confused clients.

It is possible for an organization to develop according to what seems nice on paper or in theory while, in fact, delivering the most effective services of whatever nature was appropriate to the setting. More often than not, though, a definition of structure might arise out of adherence to traditional comforts for the professional and may not develop in relation to the task at hand. Alternatively, when creating a new system, some people may learn to swim by being thrown in the water, whereas some people also drown.

A drowning staff member does not do it quickly and gracefully but does a great deal of damage to himself, other staff, and clients while he is so indisposed. Thus, a firm, supportive and broadly flexible supervisory system must exist to offer that degree of supervision and training that staff requires. There must be enough communication and definitive supervision to identify from the beginning who may need to have the reins tightened or is in need of increased supervision and structure.

While reasonable controls in the form of appropriate supervision was indicated, the formation of a supervisory system may give rise to a particularly dangerous situation – overcontrol. Overcontrol can have an extremely deleterious effect on staff functioning. When there is too much supervision, one message received by a staff is that they are not competent. They may also become afraid of making mistakes; as happens when control is excessive and creates an environment in which blame is a central consideration. In these circumstances the staff members feel that they must have their every move validated, and this cannot be done when they are dealing directly with clients. Thus, they receive and believe the message that they cannot be trusted and are incompetent. The real danger is that they then become, in fact, incompetent.

When there is no end in sight to the cases entering the clinic, and staff may fall heir to depression, anxiety, self-doubt, psychosomatic illnesses, and numerous other indicators of stress. Thus, the administrator not only is obligated to make his staff perform their functions but also must be charged with assessing their continuing well-being and mental health.

The responsibility for the well-being of a staff includes careful screening before hiring to ascertain the motivation for seeking the job. Romanticism has already been touched upon as inappropriate and general danger signals relating to insecurity, anxiety, and pathological overcommitment should be observed.

There also had to be a willingness, when the time was right, to discuss staff fears about their work environment. It was pointless to dwell on the dangers inherent in the inner city environment, but when such concerns were surfacing they had to be discussed. Staff may take pride in not being fearful of the people or the environment and still harbor fears they consider it inappropriate to express. I found it desirable to make it clear that no one was expected to make nighttime visits and certainly no one was expected to visit the top floor of a high-rise public housing project after dark on the day welfare checks were delivered. Such a trip would have been nothing other than foolhardy, and the administration had an obligation to make their expectations clear in regard to such matters as may relate to staff safety.

This condition also demanded that the staff have clearly defined backup services. Any clinical staff member in the inner city is under more than sufficient pressure to perform the basics of the job without having to hound other staff for medication, inpatient space, or whatever is needed.

Staff members had the right to expect that many things would be done for them. Morale would be seriously impaired if time and effectiveness were whittled away by numerous small issues created by administration that generated total frustration. For example, their paychecks should come at a regular time, at a regular place, and there must be provision for providing immediate information in regard to changes in the amount of money received. They also needed to know that when they need another pad of paper or a pencil that it will be there and not require six months and a pint of blood to receive it. Similarly, they wanted to be assured that their broken chair will be replaced, the lights repaired, and the heat turned on again quickly should someone forget to pay the bill. Whenever staff personnel come to question the competence of the people in the central office on such issues, they come to question their competence and responsibility in general – and correctly so.

There was also a responsibility to the staff to foster career ladders and appropriate remuneration for the job performed. Clearly career ladders were needed for community people hired by the program, but there also needed to be appropriate places for the professional staff.

Some of the staff of the Program ran out of rungs on the ladder quickly. They also experienced an inequity in remuneration when the positions of unit directors were filled by social workers and nurses. A social worker was typically paid less for the same job formerly performed by a psychiatrist (in part maybe because the social worker was more likely to be female). If they were, indeed, doing the same job, then they deserved the same pay. We are still fighting for this principle.

While discussing staff management, there is the important matter previously mentioned, related to Black professionals, that requires mention again. It became clear to me that even Black staff who occupied professional positions felt that they often could not derive intrinsic pleasure in their job because they did not know for what reasons they were hired or promoted. It was too often fashionable to place a Black person in the front office for the sake of appearances. Such continuing discrimination and racist treatment was patently obvious but distressingly common.

We often dealt with such issues as In one instance the need arose for a Black male, skilled in therapy, who could aid in dealing with a population of Black adolescents without having to spend a great deal of time learning their mannerisms, language, and customs. In another case there came a point where the facility was almost exclusively staffed by women and there was no shortage of skilled women applying, particularly in social work positions. Even under such conditions it could appear sexist to decline women who at other times would have been welcomed, but it became a necessity.

However, there were times when recommendations for staff decisions were debated on "political" grounds. Since the service area was considered by some (incorrectly) to be a Black area, one group felt that it was better to "educate" the community and that units in Black areas should be headed by Whites and units in White areas headed by Blacks. The second opinion was that Blacks should serve Blacks and Whites should serve Whites. The third position, which was my own, was that the choice should relate solely to competence and requisite skills, within reason.

"Educating the community" did not appear to be a relevant consideration in an already well-integrated staff. We were willing to accept a staff person on his own merits if he performed needed services in a capable fashion. Otherwise, a Black professional might be unable to divine whether he or she had been chosen by virtue of capacity or skin color.

Thus, one of the most overlooked functions of the administrator lay in particular kinds of management of his staff. Such management comprised much more than routine supervision, control and direction. The administrator needed to be aware of creating an environment which enhanced professional and personal growth for the staff. The means to do this may depend upon the relative maturity of the organization and the recognition of the differences in the type of staff working at any given level. Out of this process grew a realization of how to continuously develop staff functioning and assure the supportive services necessary for them to perform their functions effectively. Their position became more than a "job" to the benefit of their clients and themselves.

PHASES OF ORGANIZATIONAL DEVELOPMENT

When administrators achieved some perspective on the uniqueness of staff members as individuals differing markedly in skill, talent, and personality (even within a given profession), they could recognize the flow inherent in the life of an organization. Such an understanding also revealed how the members of that organization could relate to what was probably a unique setting, with unique tasks, and the particular problems of service delivery.

By plan or happenstance, the kinds of people hired at the beginning of the Program differed from those hired when the program was more mature. The "warm body" concept of hiring was completely inappropriate inasmuch as a new program must begin with generalists who were capable of tolerating considerable ambiguity and could proceed with a detailed assessment of the respective assets and liabilities of the community to which the program must relate. Staff had to step into numerous roles for brief periods of time. If we had hired people who needed a clearly defined niche, the program would have faltered because energy would have been spent managing the needs of the staff member rather than performing essential job functions. Specifically, in the beginning, community organization skills were just as important as clinical skills.

In the beginning of the community mental health movement, no group could plan in a smoke-filled room (yes, we had them then) and take the final product of the theoretical gymnastics out into the community and make it work well. Paper knowledge of key individuals in a community and the way the community and the primary service agencies operated was virtually useless. Instead, staff had to be dispatched on fact-finding missions to ascertain in reality what resources existed, who was who, and what things were really like. Then some reasonable priorities could be set utilizing the early, limited budget. Staff enthusiasm in this early period was considerable and at the staff level was recognized as an invaluable asset.

As the organization began to mature, its structure began to harden and the administrator had to attend to the natural desire of staff for territory. The original cadre of professionals who were attracted by challenge, newness, uniqueness, and ambiguity began to drift away. If their job had been done well, they left behind a working knowledge of the community, services were well developed, and there was a body of knowledge that enabled new staff to know whom to go to for what outside the Program. Developing methods and solving the essential problems of relating to the community had to be achieved within the first two or three years because the increasing need for structure and attention to service inevitably led the Program to turn inward.

As the services and organization became better defined, the wheel spin of the generalist who chafed at definition and management had to be eliminated. When they left, they were replaced with competent specialists who wished to relate to a specific job. These specialists' abilities lay in a different sphere and related to sound continuing development in a considerably less ambiguous environment, on which they focused particular attention.

Thus, in this community mental health organization we went through three distinct phases. First, there was the early development in which generalists were employed and the unique aspects of the community were assessed. In the first phase the particular form of each service began to develop. Second, the generalists began to leave as the organization became more tightly organized around well designed and appropriate services. New staff came with particular expertise applied to a definitive setting. Thirdly, the program reached maturity, when the balance of the program was clearly defined and operational, although some new groundbreaking on different kinds of services continued. Throughout all three periods, no matter what kind of staff was employed, the administrator had to be distinctly aware of the kind of people who were best for the particular stage of development of the program.

PROGRAM ORGANIZATION

As much as we would like to, in the abstract, no one could designate the exact form of organization of the Program. The organizational form chosen was a function of funding dictates combined with the realities of the setting. Thus, I will not dwell upon how the Program should have been organized except in relation to two issues which I found to be of paramount importance.

Autonomy Versus Central Control

Early on, the character of the Program director and key individuals tended to become the character of the organization. In this instance, considerable autonomy was established. This Program had numerous scattered facilities, and there seemed to be an inevitable autonomy of functioning in each, which was essential inasmuch as units were relating to different kinds of communities with different assets and liabilities. Those persons responsible at that level had to be given considerable autonomy to make use of the information at their disposal in designing the form and focus of that unit and their relationship with their community.

A good example of how general policy emanating from the central office was inappropriate emerged when the staff was instructed to form clinic work around groups of patients as much as possible. This approach worked somewhat in one highly stable community which was largely composed of working-class families. In the setting that I directed, we found it to be a disaster. It quickly became obvious that the best way to rid the clinic of troublesome patients was to refer them to a group, which they would not attend. It was almost magical how easy it was to decrease caseloads even when there was the best intention of forming viable groups based on careful selection.

Similarly, the type of agency that was a worthwhile focus of consultation in one area was sufficiently disorganized and withholding of services in another setting to make effective consultation impossible. The relationships with outside agencies had to be developed depending upon the realities in a given setting. Thus, there had to be some reasonable freedom to choose the agencies to receive consultation.

However, autonomy in a mental health program should not include freedom from evaluation of effectiveness. Choices should have been justified and a mutual understanding reached as to the worth of the given endeavor in that particular setting. If there was too much freedom of choice and no evaluation of effectiveness, then there was the distinct possibility of the staff embarking on never-ending dreamy projects that failed to become solidified and led to a long string of failures. Such freedom was unfair to the staff since the dreamy eyes will sooner or later become bleary eyes. It behooved the administrator to maintain close enough contact and enough long term perspective to be able to identify what was ground breaking and what was aimless shoveling.

The obviously basic points in regard to central control versus unit autonomy may fail to be obvious in the context of a high-pressure job. There was no possibility of wasting time on new projects if the organization was rigidly and traditionally controlled, but then nothing new happened, either, and the staff plodded along doing the same things that had been done for decades while avoiding relating to the community at large and its needs. People took chances when a unique design was formulated; for such an undertaking required opportunism, a willingness to give new ventures time to develop, and hardheaded but benevolent assessment of success or the reasons for failure. There would be failures and they might be monumental, but nobody learned anything if nothing was tried.

Adhocracy Versus Bureaucracy

Alvin Toffler brought a new word to wide attention when he spoke of adhocracy as contrasted with bureaucracy. His example related to the aerospace industry, where engineers might be assembled from various departments for varying periods of time to attack new problems. Personnel were assigned as a function of the particular task at hand and of their special expertise.

Effective functioning in consultation in a community mental health center may occur when the unique abilities of staff are used in an adhocratic fashion. Staff may be pulled in an opportunistic fashion from across organizational lines for a particular job. Not only may staff make opportunistic choices in regard to agencies receiving consultation but there may also be opportunistic choices of staff to embark on consultation activities. One individual might be excellent in one setting and terrible in another.

The tendency of the Program to function as an adhocracy was anathema to the bureaucracies of the State and the NIMH. During site visits they expected to see a rigid organizational chart with people droning away under fixed labels. On the whole they liked the consultation activities they saw in operation but yearned for a discrete and well-defined consultation service which they felt was de rigeur. Given my strong feeling that consultation most typically cannot be embarked upon without a service lure, I found it difficult to see how there might be a truly effective discrete service. Those persons embarking on consultation had to be prepared to pick up cases directly and not pass them on down the line in such a fashion that it might endanger a tenuous initial relationship. Thus, staff had to be able to move between the functions of clinician and consultant.

It was possible, however, to have some people engaged exclusively in consultation, but not many. I found it considerably better to embark on the high risk – high yield approach of mixing functions and making assignments on the basis of ability, not paper descriptions of functions. That is to say, the staff remained performing the basic job for which the Program was funded but would receive other assignments in a nonbureaucratic (adhocratic) fashion when the situation demanded it.

At the beginning of such a program, it would almost surely have to have a character of adhocracy rather than bureaucracy because the staff must take advantage of the new situation and there was probably insufficient staff to be wholly discrete in services. As the organization matured, it almost surely would have an increasingly bureaucratic character. Adhocratic functioning might endure in specific circumstances.

Thus, in the Program, a person might have two or three supervisors depending upon the assignment. In the clinical area he might relate to one person about clinical cases and in regard to consultation he might have two different supervisors for two different endeavors. I came to feel that such functioning was eminently more effective and that rigid refusal to make short term or varying assignments in a changing setting was the best way to stifle movement and create an unresponsive system.

PLANNING AND EVALUATION

Planning for the ongoing development of the Program was clearly a major responsibility of the central administration, even though much of the basic work was delegated to units or subunits. A glaring problem in our program was the absence of an effective research and evaluation unit from the very beginning. The Program was to have been a laboratory and was breaking new ground.

At the outset, an evaluation unit could have developed a data-gathering system by which the program could have monitored its effectiveness. It would also have been helpful for such a unit to work closely with community organizers who were shaping the picture of the community. Such a unit could have supplied the administration with the necessary data to evaluate growth and to shape development. It also could have been used creatively to develop in-house documents describing agencies, their functioning and Program relationships with them. It would have supplied crucial data to justify expenditures to the funding sources. No matter what the difficulty in obtaining a picture of services, almost everyone likes to see something which looks like hard data.

Generally speaking, in such situations, the administration plays a key role in utilization of research and evaluation activities and has to recognize not only its uses but also its shortcomings and possible abuses. Some administrators prefer not to have such a unit at all unless it can be really definitive, which it cannot be. They do not want to make public statistics that they do not understand and which may require explanation, interpretation, and defense. Thus, they muddle along with no data, asking others to accept them and their program at face value. Data can serve them, however, in justifying services to higher-ups and funding sources as well as needed documentation of a developing field where the publication of findings may be of general interest. The art is found in the evaluation and how the data is used. Often definitive outcomes cannot be identified or supported.

The administration must attend to the form in which the evaluative data is put. For example, the Program tended to define an emergency as being something that could not wait and had to be dealt with by certain designated staff. Other programs tended to include in their emergency statistics anyone who came without an appointment and desired service on the spot.

Since the Program's outpatient services were organized so that a majority of people came initially without appointments and could drop in unexpectedly even after treatment was begun, the staff did not view most of these visits as genuine emergencies. There were no waiting lists, so emergencies could not be defined in terms of whether the person was put on a waiting list or not. Thus, the Program statistics took a different form from other programs funded by NIMH.

In such a situation the administrator had to know how reported categories were defined and be willing to defend the conception of them when questioned about lower or higher rates for certain categories. It might be that insensitivity on the part of outside officials required an expedient redesigning of the methods of compiling statistics to conform more closely to the reporting of other programs. In any event, the existence of an evaluation unit would have meant somewhat more work for the administrator, but it would have paid off in the long run in the assessment of program effectiveness, defense of the program, and development of services.

Using data effectively means not using statistics to bludgeon staff unfairly. It must be recognized and communicated to the staff that it takes time being needed to get new services operational and effective. If the staff comes to feel that initial reporting will be responded to negatively, then they become timid or "fudge" their statistics. When data are handled and interpreted incorrectly, the service staff may realistically be afraid of it.

In the long run, planning is a rather extensive operation that bears on the success of the individual organization and the field as a whole. The administrator must be willing to defend his program, with the best data possible, but he must also be willing to avoid the pitfall of overselling his program and the methods of his staff.

EXTRA-ORGANIZATIONAL ISSUES

Early thinking about community mental health suggested that it would restore or create community based services for those who had lost them or never had them. Through intervention closer to home, it was thought possible to find cases early, prevent deterioration of functioning, and prevent chronicity. Thereby, the population of the state mental hospitals could be lowered.

The Relationship with State Hospitals

It was astonishing how many public officials never seemed to have read some of the basic material relating to the possibility of lowering admissions to public institutions. They acted as if the hospitals were supposed to be emptied within two or three years. They failed to remember that the original conception involved a desire to decrease state hospital populations by 50% over twenty years.

By failing to relate to reasonable goals and seeing lower state hospital admission rates as an immediate goal, they might have created a situation where fledgling community mental health programs would have become hopelessly burdened with chronic state hospital populations. If the programs became overloaded with chronic patients, there was the danger that nothing more would happen than changing the site of the same old type of treatment. And then, of course, the hospitals feared for their funding if admissions were lowered dramatically. The climate militated against a cooperative exploration of possibilities that might have worked.

There were legitimate issues regarding the design of mental hospital services. A variety of alternatives could have been evaluated.

- Smaller in-town hospitals could have been established.
- The chronic population could have been monitored after discharge by less expensive, less highly educated people hired from the communities.
- These workers could have interfaced with the community mental health staffs.
- Smaller out-of-town hospitals could have been maintained for the most serious cases.

- There could have been a graded system which would have permitted movement between smaller in-town hospitals and out-of-town hospitals.

Management in all regards would have been enhanced with these kinds of flexible efforts. Still, many other forms of preventive activities would have been needed.

With community mental health activity, hospital days might possibly have increased initially, with a decrease over time as preventive operations were given time to work. Realistically, though, the forces impacting the inner city population including epidemic drug abuse plagues like the crack epidemic, would have continued to push up chronicity of all kinds.

We will never know, but it might be that in spite of all the efforts, many sections of large cities would have continued to deteriorate. I recently returned to the neighborhood in which I used to work. I found the building that had housed our outpatient clinic. It was boarded up and the neighborhood had deteriorated markedly.

One thing is clear. Our society has lost its resolve to care for the most unfortunate. Especially among so-called conservatives, dedication to charity and understanding regarding the less fortunate seems to have virtually disappeared.

The original thinking about the long-term impact of community mental health services might have been essentially correct, but another fifteen years was needed to find out if it could be done. We never found out. Funding was slashed and the mentally ill were relegated to the streets. We no longer had a hospital problem; we had a homelessness problem.

Public Relations

At the time, having a public relations component was a relatively new idea. One way to alert the community to the existence of services was to see to it that it got mentioned in the media. But PR was an activity which required careful planning and implementation.

Public relations too often had a role in the development of a negative relationship with the state mental hospital. The negative image of the treatment of the chronic mentally ill patient often came up, either by an ill-advised comparison by staff or in a query from the media.

Likewise, it was tempting to engage in puffery. Selling services in the media made staff feel good and reflected their enthusiasm, but too often promises were made that could not be fulfilled. Image building was one thing, professional puffery another. Professionals sometimes ended up looking more like politicians or someone selling slice-and-dice appliances on television. It was essential to carefully think through the basic functions public relations should serve.

We recognized that we did not require a full fledged PR operation. We needed someone to prepare basic brochures on the Program for distribution to the community and related agencies. Also, there were numerous inquiries about the Program from within the catchment area, the city, and even from well outside the area. Someone with time to devote to it must be available to answer inquiries and organize and expedite visits when they were desired. The main thing was to have information and answers available, preferably in the hands of someone who was prepared to use them rather than sending out a naive clinician to spread the word.

Additionally, having the staff handle interviews for the media sometimes did not go well. One of my staff was very pleased with an interview she had given a local newspaper. The next day she was less happy with the headline in the newspaper reading, "Anxiety Causes Mental Illness".

Receiving Consultation

While our administrators were supposedly apprised of and critical of the consultation being given by our staff, they also were supposed to monitor consultation which the program was to receive or might want to receive. I am referring to consultation for periodic staff training or discussion of program development in the light of new federal funding or programs. Such consultation needed to be assessed very carefully; consultation was too often of the wrong sort and that the effort was wasted because little work was done to prepare for it and afterwards virtually nothing was done with the information received.

And then there was a fundamental question: Given that the community mental health enterprise in its form at the time was new, where were experienced consultants to come from?

Too often when consultants or speakers came in to advise us they had distinct agendas for pressing a method that they had found beneficial in a setting quite unlike ours. Usually neither side did any preliminary work to ensure that some benefit could be derived from the experience, such as exploring what the differences might be and why the consultant's points might or might not be applicable.

Further, I found that the NIMH tended to send cadres of "consultants" who frequently appeared to have had no firsthand experience themselves, were learning, and frequently knew less than the staff to whom they were talking. Their presentations were often insulting to an experienced "line" staff.

Let me offer you an example. The director of the Program received information that there was the possibility of NIMH personnel coming to discuss issues of community participation. Because there was a considerable lack of clarity about what the NIMH expected and what the Program wanted in its relations with the community at that time, it was apparently decided that the visit would be beneficial.

There was evidently no prior work on this subject either within the staff or by the NIMH consultants to define the form of the interchange or what might need clarification in advance. Accordingly, the group arrived and was dominated by one man who delivered what amounted to harangues in favor of community participation and seemed to pressure for community control. No information of any definitive nature was supplied on solutions to community participation problems found by other programs or the nature of the NIMH position. After the session was over, because of the irrelevance and uselessness of the interchange, no work was or could be done by the Program on the problems involved in community participation.

Ideally, once the possibility for consultation on this issue was known, the Program staff should have held meetings to define their concerns and what they desired, being as definitive as possible. This information could have been supplied to the consultants in advance so that they could have related to the unique problems of the Program. Consultation could clearly have included how other programs solved their problems and how other programs failed to develop worthwhile community participation. Ideally, the consultants could have supplied the best information available on the wishes of the NIMH even if they had not developed a clear position. It would have been at least possible to state the direction of their thinking and what they found beneficial. After the session with the consultants, the staff could have developed its own working sessions to make decisions on policy and implementation.

Unless the consultation had some concrete effects in such a situation, it was largely worthless. I felt that the administration of a community mental health center had the obligation to utilize consultants effectively or not to enter into such a contract if there was no plan or intent to build upon the new information or knowledge.

Relating to a Portion of a Whole

Extraorganizational problems are important in any setting but they take on a greater urgency when the program is located in an urban area of the kind described. Although there may be a tendency for society to ignore the problems of the poor and the inner city, the catchment area cannot be worked with as if it were an isolated island. The health, welfare, and policy systems do not confine their attentions to only one area of a city but are usually charged with a role throughout the city; some activities may even relate to the metropolitan area as a whole. Yet, such a broad and diverse area was not within the scope of one community mental health program alone.

Cities of modest size - 50,000 to 100,000 people - are attractive to workers in social services. They tend to be "graspable" in that the primary helping systems can be dealt with effectively as total entities. Similarly, a rural county formed into one community mental health target area is also quite graspable. Health services personnel can get to know the city council or county commissioners, or the police chief or the sheriff. The heads of agencies would be well known and it would be quite reasonable to work with an entire agency. Such is not and was not the case in a large urban center like Baltimore. Not even one major agency could be within the grasp of a single community mental health program.

In a small city or county area, developing a good relationship with governing officials or the personnel of other service agencies makes it possible to have signal successes – or signal failures. If serious mistakes are made, there is virtually nowhere else to go. It is easier to see major effects.

The danger for a program in the inner city, then and now, is that a staff or staff member can make remarkably bad decisions and serious errors might remain hidden. I knew that it was possible for a poorly functioning person to move on to another agency or even another section of an agency. It was this possibility that had to be monitored by the administration of a program. Sooner or later the failures would come to wider attention because, although the atmosphere was rather impersonal, there was the grapevine.

Although the Program could not relate to the police department as a whole, the interactions with the police were fruitful. We learned about the problems they were having and their frustrations in dealing with the mentally ill. By being nonjudgemental with them we at least gained mutual respect.

Frustrations occurred when there were attempts to work with judges sitting in the municipal courts located in each district. It was not reasonable to send representatives to court sessions and then only be able to accept 10 to 20% of the cases that the judge wished to refer for help because the court related to population groupings considerably too large for the Program to manage.

Granted, a program was not bound absolutely to handle only cases from its catchment area, but there were limits to the number of special agreements that could be made without overextending a staff. The situation was further exacerbated by the fact that the judges rotated through the municipal courts in the city on a monthly basis. Thus, assigned staff would have had only one month to begin to work with a judge who would then rotate out and quite possibly not return for over a year. Judges could be educated to the purposes of the community mental health effort only with great difficulty, and once out of the service area, they might well forget the subject entirely. Similarly, the police serving in one district were frequently changing assignments, so continuity could not be assumed.

Later there was a change in the police districts to form one district covering the vast majority of the catchment area. It was then possible to offer services to anyone coming before the court for that district. This much more workable situation enabled judges, over a long span of time, to become acquainted with the possibilities for assistance.

At this time, the Program was the only community mental health program operating in Baltimore and could share no work with anyone else. In sites where a number of programs existed, shared effort could have overcome these kinds of problems.

SUMMARY

There was nothing magical about community mental health administration. The administrator was responsible for meeting grant requirements and designing effective, efficient, and economical services. His responsibility included maximizing the effectiveness of the staff through growth and development of their skills and their dedication. However, in any new endeavor there is also the matter of art. It was unfortunate at the time that there were no systems for training in advance or consistent training on the job for people undertaking such responsibilities. Too frequently mental health personnel become ostriches as administrators because the people who were clinically oriented were awed by the responsibilities of a form of operation for which they were not trained.

Chapter 6
Advisory Boards

CONTEXT

There was absolutely nothing about advisory boards in my training. And there was no firm policy established by the Program. We thought we should have one or some. We didn't even know what an advisory board really was.

All I knew was that I had just come from North Carolina and for the first time in my life had experienced segregation and racial hatred of a form I had not seen. I had come face-to-face with just how disadvantaged people could be. It led me to conclude that there had to be a place for an advisory board in the inner city of Baltimore.

As mentioned, my right arm was Roz Griffin, a Black social worker. She cautioned me about advisory boards and mentored me. She never steered me wrong. We had to try to involve representatives of the inner city population in working for their future but it wasn't going to be easy.

"Maximum feasible participation of the poor" became the key words for the guidance of mental health programs in poverty areas when the federal government was attempting to promote institutional change through requirements attached to funding. For community mental health programs there was pressure to form some kind of boards but the guidelines for their operation and the powers they were to have were largely left unclarified.

Some people felt maximum feasible participation was too weak and claimed that the poor should have control over the funds entering their area for their supposed benefit. In the other camp were those who jealously guarded their professional prerogatives and and chose to see maximum feasible participation as being tokenism at most and probably no feasible participation at all.

In the middle ground between these two positions lay the advisory board chosen by the Program. This chapter will be devoted to the particular experience of the Program with the board, how it benefited the Program and the community, and the issues in developing a board of indigenous consumers or potential consumers.

THE FORM CHOSEN BY THE PROGRAM –
THE WHOLLY INDIGENOUS BOARD

The Program staff always worked with an advisory board made up of people indigenous to the catchment area and its environs. Aside from modest pressure from the NIMH, there were a number of reasons why this type of board was chosen. The motivation of higher administrative personnel for the development of the board was essentially negative. It related to a desire for window dressing and was subject to outside political pressure. My motivation related to a genuine desire to help to create a body beneficial to the Program and the community. Such a board, I felt, was an essential part of an educational program for the community.

In developing the board, numerous individuals were contacted, and even if they did not accept membership, they made the acquaintance of a Program representative and learned something of its purpose. Those individuals who came to sit on the board gathered in-depth information and talked about the work and purpose of the Program to other individuals and community groups of which they were members.

A second very positive function of the board was to provide the staff with information on such matters as the community view of needed services, the reputation of the Program in the community, and how the services were being received and might be improved. Thus, the exchange was genuinely two-way and benefited both the representatives of the community and the staff.

The reality was that many board members were former clients or had existing relationships with staff, and such a situation had distinct disadvantages. At first it was difficult to get them to express themselves. But we had to have existing relationships to bring people in and we had to go with what we had.

The general ways in which staff and community representatives learned about each other were valuable in themselves. But there was also an unforeseen political function. For example, the advisory body served well when a defense of the Program was necessary. They had a distinctly valuable role in overseeing a valued service for their community and aiding its development while having some effect in checking extraneous and inimical political forces. The existence of conservative, if not hostile, mental health forces in the state hierarchy made it important that board members were available for intervention at the interface with other institutions. In short they were the allies of the staff when we had to deal with a disinterested if not hostile University and State.

Lastly, an indigenous board was chosen out of naivete and romanticism. Given the orientation of some state officials and some university personnel, it was desirable and seemed possible to balance their orientation with a board composed of community residents. At the beginning, a romantic viewpoint about the skills and influence of a board of consumers prevailed. The initial predilections seemed to have been based on a somewhat exaggerated conception of their abilities and there was considerable naivete about their ability to hold their own in confrontation with skilled professionals who were experienced in managing mental health programs. This is not to say they were not able to pinpoint duplicity, but when the State created a superordinate body of its own to plan for the Program, it became clear that in all probability the working sessions on budgets and management would be difficult for our board. This problem suggested that a slightly different composition of the board might have been desirable (more about that later).

The history of the development of the board for the Program is properly divided into two stages – early and late. In the early stage of its development there was no clear mandate for its existence from the director, state officials, the University, or even the NIMH. Without a mandate, clear goals and guidelines it was difficult for those persons working to develop the original board to set appropriate agendas. Partly because of failure of the administration to control other staff not directly responsible for the board's creation, it became another staff meeting. As time wore on, it increasingly had the character of group therapy for some of the residents as well as staff because without a mandate an effective agenda was difficult to establish. Their most useful role at that time was participation in community fairs and other events as informational and public relations personnel.

Ultimately the failing body was dealt what amounted to a death blow by key Program staff who decided, without consulting board members, to split the board into separate units which were to be developed in relation to each outpatient satellite center and not in regard to the entire program. Needless to say, such an independent move on the part of the staff was in no way diplomatic. The lack of a mandate and generally muddled thinking on the part of the highest levels of the Program staff were largely responsible for this unfortunate decision.

The later phase of the development of the board began at this point. Although as a unit director I was not mandated to create a board, it was clear that I was free to work for one, and I came to believe that its development was desirable if not essential. Based on what was essentially a passive mandate to develop a board relating to the satellite I directed, Roz and I undertook its development.

Using expanded lists of "community leaders" and capable individuals, we set out to assemble it. Whatever time could be stolen from clinical duties was used to contact people previously unconnected with the Program. Finally, when the time for meetings to begin approached, former stalwart members of the board residing in the area were contacted. Toward the end of the summer there were enough interested people to begin meetings, and by then there was a slightly firmer mandate in that NIMH was indicating that they considered an advisory board highly desirable and hoped to see evidence of one when the next site visit was made. The staff of the other operational satellite facility continued to show virtually no interest in a board of their own.

Initially the meetings were directed by two staff persons, but our intent was to lessen control and influence by the staff as leaders emerged. Because it was essential to avoid previous mistakes, the participation of the satellite staff was severely limited and it was clearly stated they would be invited guests at times when it was essential and desired by board members. The two staff persons became resource people, although early on it was necessary for them to take a strong hand in the organization of the board. Gradually the staff was able to move into the background and relinquish control.

At last the staff became informationally oriented professionals who represented the Program. They also assumed the role of nonvoting observers. However, assuming a less central posture for staff was made difficult by vacillation on the part of the administration. They failed to discourage staff from coming to board meetings at will for whatever purpose they wished. Still, the board was growing stronger and at this point they reformed themselves into an advisory board for the entire program.

After the initial period of development, two primary goals were identified. First, it seemed desirable to incorporate the body to make its members independent and make it possible for them to receive funds should such an opportunity arise and, second, the employment of community residents in the Program was long overdue in view of the growing maturity of the Program. We collected petitions from the community to support the latter goal and tried to engage the interest of the Program as a whole in this endeavor. The growth and development of the board was hastened by the import of these goals.

Then, fortuitously, state officials solidified the board by calling for public hearings and questioning the need for the central building which was to be constructed for the Program. Community residents became more interested and former members from the other satellite appeared to lend a hand. Being stronger, they were a crucial influence in the hearings, and a major mental health official made an impulsive commitment to seek jobs in the Program for indigenous persons. Thus, the hearings solidified the advisory board and provided an initial commitment for developing new job classifications for inner city residents.

The relative disengagement of staff and the increase of the board's independence came just in time. It became necessary to terminate a highly troublesome nonindigenous community organizer. Since he was oriented toward building a power base for his own purposes, he sought to fight for his position using the advisory board as a forum. He and another staff member with a similar orientation attempted to pack and control the board and brought in a demagogue who claimed he was the true spokesman for the "community". Although they had been previously uninterested in developing an advisory board, now, when it suited their purposes, this segment of the staff showed sudden interest in the advisory board, the well-being of the community, and support for community control. However, even though organizational restraints were not firm, the board was able to resist these moves and, by taking a neutral position, made it possible for the Program to terminate the staff member. By this time the board members were also well aware that they could not have control of the Program. There were numerous long, arduous shouting matches but in the end the board members showed the strength and commitment to weather attacks.

Although the insertion of other issues slowed their movement, the importance of the issues served to solidify the organization and the board ultimately was able to incorporate, with the assistance of a lawyer from a legal aid program. At the same time they continued to press for jobs for community residents. Despite verbalized commitments on the part of state officials, every step in the process was impeded and it took over a year for new job classifications to be formalized. Through these struggles the board members gained knowledge and were sufficiently legitimized in the eyes of the State to exercise some power in obtaining membership on a board designed by the State for shaping the form of services in the planned central building. It was in this area, as it was being developed, that they showed how well they could function and what was learned under fire.

GENERAL PRINCIPLES

The issue of community was discussed in Chapter 1 – there being no such entity except in an operational sense for a specific purpose. But anyone working in a community-oriented program will sooner or later hear, "What this community wants…". When we heard those words, we had to keep in mind that wherever human beings collect in large numbers, they will be deeply divided by special needs or wants, special status considerations, and friendship groups formed around common interests of employment, proximity of living space, goals, education, class standing, leadership skills, problems, personality, religion, etc. We knew there were numerous agendas but, realistically, many common problems. With an open mind it was possible for staff to work with people presenting themselves from the community. We were able to define needs and formulate with them the best utilization of extremely limited resources. It was important not to be used by one group for their purposes. (It should be mentioned that a special interest group may reside in the community or within the staff, as was the case in the problem with the community organizer terminated by the Program, and there may be an alliance between the two groups.)

It was difficult to accept, but, despite the best intentions, someone would inevitably be alienated. The most self-interested individual or groups would be very aggressive in pushing their demands and raise the specter of the alienation of the "entire community". While members of the staff, if they had not come to terms with their own guilt and class and racial prejudices, would tend to rush to reassure the accusing body that they were, indeed, on their side. This occurred very early in the development of the Program when staff impatient for maximum movement made exaggerated promises. In so doing, they promised what was impossible to deliver, whether it was special treatment for retarded children, jobs, or football uniforms. Acceding to such demands only postponed the inevitable deterioration of relations.

The inner city was composed in large part of individuals who had received the most negative kind of treatment in society. Whether it was from "the man", the employer, the corporation, the family, peers, or whatever, many persons had developed a hypothesis that basically indicated to them that they should expect nothing but bad treatment from other people. Their expectation of mental health professionals was similar – bad. Accordingly, giving in to the demands of the most vociferous individuals who held this negative hypothesis only led to more demands, and ultimately they succeeded in proving to themselves what they believed all along. No matter how cautious staff members attempted to be, sooner or later they would meet this type of individual as they searched through the inner city for productive alliances to solve problems. All too often these type of people were the first to arrive at the door to "check you out". In view of this possibility, it was generally appropriate to be polite and relatively noncommittal until there was time to get the organization going and develop a knowledge of community groups.

The inevitable painstaking job in beginning a mental health program included the operationalizing of the essential services and assembling the best possible network for gathering information. This network, the relationships and friendships so built, were essential to the development of a working knowledge of the target area and the optimal ways of delivering services, as well as obtaining feedback to help keep the staff honest, forthright, and vital in delivering services. Developing the widest variety of contacts also served as a distinctly useful method of educating the community about mental health and what services could realistically be delivered.

It is worth emphasizing, particularly in working in the Black community, that under pressure there was the tendency to respond to a person representing himself as a spokesman for the Black community as if he indeed represented all Black people. Unfortunately, a common assumption was that, because the professional did not grow up in a given area, he must leave at home his own ability to criticize and conceptualize problems. One particularly good example will serve.

Heroin addiction was a major problem in Baltimore, as elsewhere, and an institution near the Program serving a similar population was contemplating a treatment program for heroin addicts. A series of meetings were held to begin the formulation of the program and to prepare the grant application. The individuals attending the meetings were both professionals and paraprofessionals. The major issues did not revolve around whether to have a program or how large, (money limitations indicated that the largest program conceivably funded would not be sufficient) but, rather, the nature of the services to be delivered. As was appropriate, the interested professionals and paraprofessionals had discussed the issue among themselves before the meeting and had already achieved some reasonable consensus regarding the form of the program. One Black man in this group who was well-known for being engaged in services for alcoholics was most adamant that the only service needed was detoxification, with limited counseling and no continuing followup or maintenance on other drugs. He was definite that the Black community wanted only this kind of program and Black addicts would only accept this one type of approach. It was appalling to see so many of the professionals passively nodding assent and accepting his statement as the gospel for the Black community because he was Black, aggressive and lived in the area.

The experience of the Program staff had established the understanding that multiple options were desirable to treat heroin addiction, depending upon the particular problems of the individual and how deeply involved he was in use or traffic. This was not the primary point, however. It was the uncritical acceptance of the Black paraprofessional's statement which was at issue. Afterwards it came out that this self-proclaimed spokesman was "chipping" - was himself an occasional user of heroin. He had controlled his alcoholism but when he felt depressed or pressured he evidently turned to heroin and periodically required detoxification. It seemed apparent that he was speaking for himself; having an option for periodic detoxification and not continuing counseling or treatment, he could avail himself of such services and avoid being forced to face his own problems. Consciously or unconsciously he had an investment in helping to create a program to serve his particular needs. He did not and could not speak for a nonexistent, cohesive Black community or subcommunity.

PROBLEMS IN DEVELOPING A BOARD OF INDIGENOUS CONSUMERS

Let us lay aside the issue of community control, which will be discussed later in the chapter. For the moment the issue is an advisory board of the form chosen by the Program. The problems now to be discussed are general issues experienced in the development of the advisory board.

After overcoming the fear of loss of control to the community, the hardest part of the endeavor to obtain participation of community representatives was permitting normal group process to operate. Professionals are often impatient; they want to get organized and move toward clear objectives. Without permitting group process, an advisory group will develop either into an old ladies' knitting club (a puppet board), or an explosion.

The first step after assembling a body of the most responsive and responsible citizens, who may include moderate activists, was to educate them in the clearest possible manner as to the purpose of the program, its structure, and the limitations of their power as an advisory board. It was beneficial to help them through an examination of the grant and what it meant. The individuals properly participating in this function were current clients, former clients, or interested individuals recommended from the community. The biggest danger at that point was in allow-ing a demagogue to dominate the meetings for his own purposes. However, clear statements at the very beginning in regard to limitations for the possibility of con-trol can often discourage such an individual when he finds he will not receive con-trol or financial largesse. There was, of course, the type of individual who enjoys watching guilty liberals squirm, so it was best to be neither guilty nor squirm and possibly not be so "liberal" but rather businesslike. If a dysfunctional individual or demagogue had come to dominate the group, it would probably have died of its own polemical weight and a new beginning would have to be undertaken.

Once we had a viable body of citizens, it was necessary to direct its move-ments during the early stages. There were windy sessions and boring sessions until everyone knew everyone else's positions, and alliances began to form. This type of process was not unique to inner city residents, of course; I saw it in every con-sultation contact and every professional meeting I ever attended. As in every other group, time must be allowed for a display of each individual's interest, abilities, and philosophy, and everyone's working knowledge of the positions of other people.

As quickly as possible we developed a meaningful and interesting agenda, so that there was work to do when the complex dance of acquaintanceship was fin-ished. At that point the true leadership could begin to evolve and staff had to yield at the earliest opportunity. The board was, after all, not a creature for professional domination but needed its independence.

It was preeminently important to make it a genuine meeting of the community, with the agency staff serving as informational sources and contacts with the larger program, and not a floating quasi-staff meeting serving as a vehicle for misguided or dissident staff. This was not to say staff could not be invited by the board for specific agenda matters or to raise problems, but control needed to be exercised over the goings and comings of Program staff. Otherwise they could quickly domi-nate at the expense of the appropriate development of group process. Exclusion of staff also meant the exclusion of community people hired by the Program. There was place for them at the most basic council levels as bridge-makers if necessary, but in a central body they had clearly become staff and had separate agendas. Not incidentally, if the board was to be truly viable, it could not be dominated or swayed by voting Program staff. Control of board decisions through votes would have been highly suspect.

What the meeting also was not was group therapy. This pitfall was a mag-nificent way to satisfy the clinician who felt out of his element and would prevent meaningful work. However, it had to be recognized that participation on the advisory board was often a back-door entry to therapy. Such overtures had to be handled outside of meetings and by someone not involved with the board as soon as possible.

Sooner or later the group might take on the character of one person who would dominate. It was not desirable but very common. If it remained a functional body, then well and good, but if new blood was needed, it was within the function of the staff representatives to continue to find new members as a counterbalance. Seeking new members was both the function of community members and of staff assigned as representatives to the board. We hoped relationships were strong enough that tact could serve to tone down the domination by the key individual.

Once the group was established, had taken over its own leadership role, and was working on real and important agenda items, the arrival of new members generated another set of problems. Reasonably simple written material had to be available to orient newcomers. The best outcomes happened when staff worked together with them in a separate meeting to educate them on the functions of the agency, the functions of the board, and current agenda items and goals in context.

It was also important to remember that the meetings of an advisory board did not need to include large numbers of people. The number of active individuals in any community is limited. We considered the attendance of ten or twelve reasonably consistent and dedicated persons to indicate that things were going well. In a manner of speaking, the board was their club activity, and we were sure that they were conveying information to many other people and groups. When crises arose, this core was able to mobilize many more people.

Thus, after overcoming the fears of the administration and dealing with dictates of funding sources and professionals' reservations in general, the most important thing for the involved professional to do was to permit group process, clarify limitations, and control the staff. Mutually beneficial partnerships were quite possible and yielded the benefits already mentioned.

ALTERNATIVE MODELS

At least two other basic models for the composition of advisory boards should be mentioned here, although they were not applicable to the circumstances of the Program. First, there is what may be termed the "blue ribbon board" composed of prominent individuals with the highest level of financial and management expertise.

Such boards can supplement the professional expertise of a program and can be helpful in being "angels" bearing gifts (of money) or undertaking fund-raising activities. Unfortunately, even by flexing the Program boundaries to the maximum, the community did not contain such individuals, and it would have been inconceivable to expend the effort to interest such individuals in the Program and its catchment area.

Another form could be a board composed of mental health professionals from the entire city who would aid in developing the Program and working on its planning. It was this type of body toward which the state officials were oriented. Such a group would have been disinclined, in the prevailing professional atmosphere, to interfere with existing spheres of influence and might have inhibited the natural development of the Program. Such a board would have prevented maximum relatedness and responsiveness to the community served. It was precisely because of the underground tensions and inimical objectives of many mental health professionals that the advisory board developed in the form it did. Balance was needed.

RETROSPECTIVE ANALYSIS OF A PROBABLE BETTER ALTERNATIVE

Although the board in its original form served well under exceedingly difficult conditions and was reasonably representative of the community, its flaw related to severe limitations in dealing with professionals. It lacked sufficient critical expertise, planning abilities, budgetary knowledge, and so on to stand up in confrontations with experienced State and University personnel. The infinite variety of budget subterfuges could be hidden from them until it was too late to change an accomplished fact.

For these reasons, it might have been better to formulate at least two levels of boards. For each satellite there could have been a board composed exclusively of community residents to deal with problems specific to each satellite. Their endeavors could have been heavily weighted toward community affairs and could include educational and public relations activities at the local level. This is where they would be strongest. They could also have been helpful in pushing for improved services.

The second level could have been a superordinate body relating to the Program as a whole and weighted heavily with the elected representatives of the satellite boards. The balance of the board could have been composed of skilled professionals who worked in or related to programs for the poor. They could have been picked because of their clear commitment to the area and demonstrated importance to the community. Thus, the superordinate board would possess direct communications with the community, indirect links through other important agencies or institutions, and the crucial expertise to assess program movement, development, and political manipulations. In a healthier climate with more enlightened mental health officials, the inclusion of representatives from the State and the University could well have been indicated.

COMMUNITY CONTROL

The very first issue which we had to confront when a board was proposed was the question of community control of a program designed to deliver mental health services. Community control usually implied various forms of control of funds, direction, and administration. In an impoverished area this has the appeal of freeing the poor from the possibility for "imperialism" by professionals and permitting the poor to take control of their own destinies through the control of large amounts of money channeled into their neighborhoods for improving their lot.

Although in theory community control may sound compelling and viable, in reality it was neither possible nor desirable to give control to the community in most cases. In general, persons from the community lacked the expertise to administer the funds, and only through a working, trusting partnership could they help to shape the program. When the possibilities for abuse were considered, there was, after all, little difference between professionals slicing the pie and poor people slicing the pie. In one case, the relatively rich get richer and in the other some of the poor get less poor until the political winds shift and the funds disappear. In either case the mass of the people needing help may fail to receive qualitative services.

When an advisory board begins to meet, the poor may be incited to visions of control, while the professionals may fear loss of control, loss of status, loss of income, and loss of prerogatives. Where the fears of professionals predominate, they may be defensively disdainful of the "lower classes". Given the pressures existing in the inner city, they were gambling with chaos, insurrection (community and staff), and the possibility of a vastly weaker and pedestrian program. Such disdain evidenced a lack of confidence in themselves and what they had to offer. They failed to take account of the positive interests residing in the community and discounted the potential benefits of learning about the experiences of the poor.

I am not suggesting that professionals should have overly romanticized the unique experiences of the poor when measured against their more comfortable existences, but as professionals learned better service delivery modalities, they needed the form of expertise found in the residents' knowledge of stresses and methods of survival.

I adhered to the position that involvement of the poor as advisors and participants was not only desirable but imperative. Control by them was out of the question. There had to be an alliance between community people and Program representatives based on a free exchange of information and partnership in what should be a mutually beneficial endeavor to foster an effective and relevant program.

At times there may have been an impulse to turn over virtual control or at least a veto power to representatives of the community. The desire may have been well-intentioned, especially when a core of responsible and capable community residents was working with and advising a program staff. But a long-term perspective militated against such a decision. It would have been a particularly bad one without levels of boards that could develop well-informed indigenous people to replace advisors when inevitable attrition took place. With no provision for finding reliable and capable replacements, if a veto power had been given to the board, any vacuum very probably would have been filled with a demagogue or destructive mil itant who sensed an opportunity for personal gain or simply an opportunity to make trouble.

Thus it seemed better to have an agreement on a de facto veto. If there was trust, honesty, and a real working partnership, then, when a community representative expressed opposition, the differences could be talked out or, if it was equivocal, a search could be undertaken for another job candidate, in the case of staff recruitment, or even for another policy.

Professionals who were solely in the mental health field for the money were often deeply concerned about their status. Failing to see that everyone was enhanced by a working alliance, they felt that they would be devalued by the representatives of the community. They did not understand that these representatives often wished to revere them as a part of their (hoped for) veridical perception that they and their community were receiving qualitative services. The greatest dangers existed for the professionals who were oriented toward building empires for themselves. The more baronial, personal, and shady the empire, the more they would oppose dealing with the community. Too many professionals seemed to be abusing their positions and appeared to be mainly concerned with their income. They could not afford an open partnership.

Even conscientious professionals could unjustly resist the notion of relationships with a community concerned with the direction of the Program and the development of services. When noise by a community resident was mistaken for influence and community following and the professionals were unwilling to face the boredom, hard work, and potential harangues found in the development of a board, then the professionals abdicated their charge to develop the soundest possible program.

COMMENT

Trials and tribulations are predictably to be endured by the professional attempting to form a community-based board. However, the essential element to bring to this occasionally chaotic but often boring situation is an objective, critical faculty. A useful and effective advisory board depends upon clearly defined participation and not control. Genuine commitment to make an advisory board work on an honest basis is a distinct asset. Even for the professional who sees no clear need for such a board, when working in the inner city, it is a virtual certainty that the day will come when a well-developed partnership will "save your neck" and permit the poor to continue to have beneficial programs. Even when a poverty area is not the exclusive focus of a program, it is essential to the appropriate delivery of services to include the poor in some advisory capacity. I can conceive of no one with any breadth of vision who would not benefit from the valuable assistance of representatives of the community that he is supposedly serving. It just takes diligence and understanding to include them in the right way.

Mental health professionals, however, tend to be trained to see themselves as the exclusive proprietors of the programs in which they work. It seems very difficult for professionals to accept and understand the working partnership of an advisory board founded on deserved trust on the part of both partners. When a board is created and mismanaged or used for personal causes, it becomes a destructive influence on both the program and the community. When the board represents a viable trusting partnership, it fosters growth and balance. Although the advisory board I worked on was beset by continuous crises, its beneficial effects cannot be denied. The information from the community members proved again and again to be invaluable, and they obtained the ear of state officials, criticized racism when it appeared, and defended the Program and its funding. The greatest and longest-lasting effect aside from indirectly fostering good service should have been the creation of jobs in the State for people who might have been excluded from employment in mental health organizations. The people I termed community workers were meant to become an integral and important part of the staff and the Program. As it turned out the people hired were able to make a valuable contribution. Overall, the work to create a viable advisory board was an excruciating process but more than worth it.

Roger B. Burt

Chapter 7
Employing Residents of the Community

CONTEXT

In the inner city of Baltimore we were surrounded by terrible poverty. Jobs in the area were difficult to find, and employment often had to be sought far away in another section of the city.

With the opening of the Program, there was the possibility for jobs. Even before we had an advisory board, we had begun to develop the perspective that it was only just that we should be a source of employment for local people.

Our staff also came to hold the heretical view that, especially given our model, some services for our clients could be provided by people who were not highly trained and highly paid mental health professionals.

Among the books we were reading at the time was *New Careers for the Poor* by Riessman and Pearl. They presented reasoned arguments for bringing the poor into service agencies as employees and correctly stated that employment, particularly in the service fields, was an effective approach to affect poverty. Such employees could take over many duties formerly performed by professionals and thereby reduce the manpower shortage we had at the time. They represented a section of a mental health staff that was distinctly service-oriented and spent little if any time in research and training. As noted in the preceding chapter, some of the staff of the Program accepted these arguments, and with the assistance of the advisory board sought jobs for people from the community.

CAREER LADDERS – NEW CAREERS

Providing a job is quite different from developing a career. A job may be little more than static employment, but a career offers the potential for a rewarding existence with the opportunity to increase competence as well as additional income. The staff of the Program hoped that they would be able to offer a career to those who were hired from the community. Because of the resistance on the part of state officials, there did not immediately exist a career ladder but only an opening or entry position and the possibility for some mobility in the future.

The problem of making a career in a state system was not a problem unique to the community worker but applied to the mental health professional as well. Vertical movement was not always difficult and many of the staff, because of the newness of the endeavor and the nature of the organization, were able to move up quickly and ran out of rungs on the ladder within four years. Thus, they entered a static position.

An even more serious issue, however, was that positions were tied rigidly to education and training. With such rigidity, it was expected that duties would be in line with traditional role expectations. This situation was limiting both to the community worker and the professional alike, because personal development does not always occur along traditional lines. The potential for personal growth and fulfillment could not be found in the state system but was present in the climate of the Program, which provided experiences and roles according to personal capabilities. Thus, there was somewhat more freedom for personal and programmatic development, if not recognition in terms of a job classification. In both cases, the job could be static and the career had to be found in the flexibility of the organization.

SELECTION

We were clear who we were seeking to hire and train. We wanted people from the community we served or very nearby, and we referred to them as community workers. After the training program and the job at the other end were assured, the next issue was selection of community workers. While selection may have seemed to be a relatively simple affair, in fact, the numerous pitfalls soon become apparent.

The selection process was a natural point for the involvement of the indigenous people on the advisory board and, indeed, their contacts and viewpoints were essential to bridging the expected gap between an organization and the community.

However, their predilections tended to run to hiring themselves, their relatives, their friends, or some "poor soul who needs a job". Thus, the first rule inspired by a board member was that anyone having any relationship with an applicant must excuse himself. Secondly, the assumption had to be implanted that the desired person was the most qualified. But "qualified" did not mean the person with the most education. Rather, we sought people who showed the most promise of benefiting from training and effectively applying their natural talent. It was much easier said than done.

The first group of people avoided by the board were the professional trainees. There were numerous and competing programs for training in the inner city, and some people apparently pursued the occupation of trainee. These individuals did not necessarily enter endless rounds of training intentionally, but because of various subtle or gross disabilities (often emotional) they were unable to take advantage of training. Their lives become an endless circle of participation in training programs, welfare, recycling in training, welfare, and new training programs. A careful examination of their backgrounds and their presentation of themselves usually revealed this chronic pattern.

However, each person deserved a careful review, and prior experience and failure in a training program or training programs was not sufficient reason for automatic exclusion from consideration. Some training programs were poorly designed and, in fact, did not help the person gain employment or at least did not maximize his or her chances to benefit from training. The former trainee may genuinely have been victimized. It was our job to know enough about the community to be able to see who might have been victims.

It also became clear to the people involved in selection that the school system fairly routinely failed to counsel its students well. In some cases high school graduates were interviewed who had taken a curriculum that prepared them for nothing in particular and who could not find any acceptable job. Such a person clearly needed a chance for getting job-directed training or at least decent counseling to permit a productive job search. Some job applicants with some background in college had not received any guidance to help them find employment. The nature of their educational experience and the lower-class attributes (their "rough" edges) and the contrast with middle-class applicants with whom employers were comfortable made them poor last choices in the eyes of potential employers. Even when employed, they were often underemployed.

There were many applicants for community worker positions, and many individuals who were not chosen. It was a rare opportunity to screen a large number of individuals who would not ordinarily have come to the attention of a mental health organization. Some could be helped to find the appropriate resources. It was appalling to discover how many people were simply not getting to the available resources that could offer them help of potentially great benefit. Many of them were excellent candidates for focused programs selected by a vocational rehabilitation counselor.

The Program learned the hard way that no other agency should be given anything approaching exclusive responsibility for finding applicants. Other agencies often made incorrect assumptions as to who was needed. Or the class and racial balance among those persons referred might differ from the composition of the catchment area. At times they had their own target groups that they wished to prevail upon the program to accept. While good people might come from such contacts, it was crucial for our mental health organization to make its wishes clear. An initial overreliance on other agencies to find applicants made the board's job more difficult, but they were nevertheless able to find good applicants.

Even when our mental health program retained control over outreach, some agencies did us a disservice. For example, the personnel of one training program made a great deal more work for the people reviewing applicants by mishandling the announcement of job opportunities. After receipt of the information, one of the staff members of the training program simply walked into a room filled with people in orientation and without explanation told them to go to the Program because there were jobs available. The trainees had no notion of the kind of job available or of the minimal requirements. When they came to be interviewed, they were often bewildered; some of them would not have applied if they had known the duties of the job. This agency was clearly not being responsible to its enrollees and endangered the future use of their services.

While talking with the applicants it was necessary to be very clear as to what was being offered and to be realistic and not promise training toward specific ends, which might not be possible, or mobility, of which there was no assurance. Many persons did not ask what the job was about but simply tried to present a good face in hopes of finding a job to which they might adapt themselves. Such individuals were not necessarily the worst candidates but, rather, were often not in the position of having any other options. In view of this tendency to be uncritical or to fail to ask appropriate questions, a strong reality position was indicated and the interviewers were forced to anticipate the questions the applicants might wish to ask or should have asked.

Roger B. Burt

EMPLOYMENT AT THE BEGINNING OF A NEW PROGRAM

Initially, the Program staff had no experience in hiring community workers. Hiring them at the beginning of the Program would have yielded distinct benefits. Everyone would have been infected by the initial esprit de corps, and new professional staff would have gotten an assist in getting oriented to the community.

However, in reality, position descriptions had to be established according to properly defined roles, training systems had to be designed and ready, the state system (as applicable in the case of the Program) had to have a classification for them, and the applicants had to have some assurance of mobility (i.e. having a future with the organization).

Early hiring would have meant there were no heavy clinical caseloads, and the initial orientation as to the purpose and goals of the Program would have been more leisurely. All levels of staff could have gotten acquainted together. The paraprofessionals could have begun to contact and educate the community to the purposes of the Program, make contacts in seeking cases, and go to other poverty-related agencies to develop contacts and referral sources. The best advantage would have been that everyone would have been starting off learning together. Morale would have been maintained and developed while their training in clinical and community organization techniques were under way. These particular benefits were not available in the Program.

EMPLOYMENT IN AN ADVANCED PROGRAM

In this instance, the Program had been operating for over three years, and if there was one thing the staff did not need, it was more clients. Thus, we had to develop opportunities for the community workers to work with staff while their training continued. Bringing in a new classification of employees was a struggle at the beginning. Uniformly, the new staff members knew when they were receiving busy-work, and morale was a problem. They could not be sent on case-finding ventures without experience, but it was possible to initiate them into case assistance and consultation work and to provide them with an observational role in appropriate clinical settings.

In fact, the community workers could have been put to work directly with the cases the staff referred to as "maintenance" cases. These people needed regular contacts and often dogged work. The professional staff, without considering the consequences, was tempted to pass these cases on to the community workers. Doing so would have severely limited their role, if that was all they ever did. Rather, the decision was made to hold their role with maintenance cases to a minimum to ensure that community workers had the time to develop other skills. This decision required constant monitoring by the staff because it was too easy to forget about our fledgling employees. It worked because the staff was serious about developing a broad role for the community workers even though it meant continuing some boring work themselves and required continuous vigilance.

Unfortunately, although the selection process went reasonably well, the first year of training community workers and their initial experience with the Program can only be termed a disaster. Enthusiastic people were received into the Program and were substantially mistreated as the result of administrative vacillation. The ensuing events were largely a function of ill will on the part of some staff and taught us nothing except how not to proceed.

The training was funded under a federal grant that provided money for academic upgrading, including courses to prepare the trainees for gaining their high school equivalency certificates and monies for specifically related college training for those persons who had finished high school. The institution that got the money had no experience in effective training of disadvantaged people and provided few resources for a meaningful program. Because of the weakness in the central administration, it took most of an academic year to change a situation, which was quite evidently bad from the beginning.

At the same time, components of their training were used in such a way as to keep them separate from the rest of the staff and that led to hurt feelings and anger. They were used as a vehicle by the trainer to build a dysfunctional empire that created the feeling that the professional staff members were "against" the community workers. The romanticism and the supposed desire to keep them "fresh" were used by this person against the Program staff when attempts were made to force assessment of the workers' progress in terms of the various components of the training program.

Although much information was coming to my ears secondhand, I could not use it effectively because of administrative inaction and vacillation. At one point I was faced with a disturbing session with one of the most promising community workers choking back tears while she explained why she felt she might lose the job she wanted so badly. She feared termination during probation and did not know that I would be responsible for confirming her as a permanent employee and was looking forward to the day. I even found myself in the difficult position of trying to

124

restrain angry advisory board members who had information about the problems in the training program from different sources. All of us feared that a public crisis at that particular juncture might have brought ruinous intervention by hostile state officials. The situation was especially critical because hiring and training community workers was a pioneering endeavor in the State and the Program was being watched closely but not in a benign fashion.

Since this was basically a pathological situation, there is no point in focusing on it in detail except to point out that failure to make careful choices regarding personnel training can lead to conflict which benefits no one. Fortunately, later on some staff and advisory board members forced needed changes and the training was substantially improved.

Although an agonizing year had been wasted, training then began, along with on-the-job experience. It was too bad the initial training was so disastrous, but at least the Program did not make the common error of obtaining a training grant only to find at the end that the funding agency had failed to provide position descriptions and money for actual jobs. Eight of the original ten community workers and two replacements completed training and began full-time work in the satellites.

There were light moments along the way. My special favorite was when we set about getting newly trained community workers on the street to do follow-ups with tractable clients. We handed maps to each of them. They turned the maps around and back and forth with puzzled looks on their faces. Not one of them had any experience with reading maps. Suddenly it dawned on us; Why would they have needed to know that skill? They took numbered buses over familiar routes to communities they knew.

I did know that one of them had driven to visit relatives in Atlanta, and I asked her how she had done it. She had taken a friend who had made the trip previously. They looked for a sign to Washington, then a sign to Richmond, and so on.

So, before we could proceed with home visits, we had to have a class in map reading, and some of it had to be on the street so they could connect the map to the physical world. There were many more unanticipated classes ahead.

ROMANCE – THE NOBLE SAVAGE MYSTIQUE

A commonly stated belief in professional circles was that community workers had a unique ability to help their neighbors by virtue of being able to communicate in the same language and because they had a deeply felt understanding of common problems based on mutual experience. Although not entirely true, the belief draws on the nineteenth-century noble savage mystique. Along with this view of the community worker, there was often an implicit assumption that the person from the community would not be defensive with his comrades in misery and, because of the shared experiences, possessed unique ways of solving problems.

While the community residents might have possessed a body of experience that differed from the professionals' experience, they still required training in techniques of interviewing, intervention, and, at a basic level, understanding of what another person was really saying. They may also have come burdened with a negative view of their fellow man, a desire to rise above by trampling underfoot, extremely negative views of agencies (which might prevent their mustering enthusiasm for a referral to the best possible resource), and a general lack of faith in their own future and the future of those they were to begin serving. In short, preconceived notions were to be avoided when bringing in people from the community. They were heir to all human foibles and needed to be approached on a person-by-person basis to assess strengths and weaknesses.

Once having brought the noble savage to the bosom of the Program to be nurtured (or to nurture the professional), the next naïve assumption was that they could be made a part of the agency in such a fashion that they could somehow be trained but not changed. As desirable as it was that they avoid the failings of the professionals, they could not possibly serve a worthwhile function and not change.

Change was not bad in and of itself. If they improved their position in life, acquired new skills, and moved out of the inner city, it was hardly unfortunate. Such individuals acquired a new mobility and a higher income and, when they left, there was room for another person to grasp the rung on the ladder. Ideally, they were not imprisoned in a dead-end job but had been offered an unprecedented opportunity. If they left to take another job, they took with them their experience and the ability to bring to other people a valuable education in a wholly different setting. We did not have the option to keep community workers just as they were. They would change, in any event, and some of them would continue to develop and move up and on. Even those who would be unable to move beyond their initial functioning would be changed irrevocably, at least in their views of themselves and the world.

THE OUTCOME

It took continuing pressure to assure at least some form of a ladder so that the community workers could move beyond the entry level. Some individuals showed a potential for diverse and highly skilled functioning. While some form of a ladder and a career became a possibility in the Program, it typically took a rigid standard form of : (1) entry level, (2) more experienced, (3) supervisor, and (4) department head. For the community workers there was the possibility of multiple roles, including outreach, contacting community resources, developing community resources, community organization (or planning), consultant, and lay therapist. To recognize these as developed skills and give appropriate recognition and remuneration was nearly impossible in the state system. Some form of recognition was possible in the Program in terms of rewards accruing interpersonally from the staff and the people served.

With truly expert assistance from the advisory board, the Program was able to hire very promising people. After years on the job, the development of these people was diverse. But in general it proved to be a success. People who generally had not finished high school came to a program with little knowledge of mental health. Usually their employment had been marginal or they had been on welfare. Now they had proved themselves and validated the principles of including the poor in agencies as service personnel.

Some of the staff had entertained the hope that community workers might actually be able to take on therapeutic roles. In some cases they showed they possessed this capacity.

An even more pleasant surprise occurred with the blossoming of some of these people when they were included in work with other agencies. By being present in the atmosphere of a mental health facility and by going along on consultation work, some of them developed finely honed analytical skills which permitted them to see the complex dynamics of other agencies and to pinpoint resistances and manipulations in consultation activities.

In all, it was a very satisfactory experience, and when the problems of selection, training, and employment were hurtled, we confirmed our belief that people from the community could make substantial contributions to the mental health programs that employed them.

So, in the beginning the battles that were fought led to success and validation of the concept of employing people from the community. But, given the atmosphere and the attitudes of the state and the university personnel ,it should not be hard to guess that the long-term result was not so satisfactory.

Roger B. Burt

Chapter 8
Other Applications of the
Service Model

CONTEXT

Our small band of young professionals could not possibly have known what kind of job they were taking. But we knew the country was changing; old ways of doing things were being challenged and we wanted to be a part of the change.

Many of us had had classical training in psychotherapy and were quite well acquainted with psychoanalysis. At first, in responding to the area residents, nothing seemed to work, nothing was applicable. We felt we might as well have been inventing the wheel.

Fortunately there were social workers among us. They knew about helping people, about reaching out, and assessing a community. Together we were able to formulate an approach that worked. Some of it validated what Gerald Caplan had said and then turned out to be applicable to other populations.

We quickly learned that there were flaws in assuming that we could use a medical model in responding to our population. In fact, we never entirely resolved the issue and tended to use "client" and "patient" interchangeably. There were uses for diagnoses, especially when we were dealing with psychoses and organically based illnesses. But most of our work related to people who were trying to cope with an impossibly difficult life. Helping them with it suggested a strong preventive orientation and addressing the reality of their existence. As it turned out, the model we derived had utility with other populations.

AN APPLICATION TO ANOTHER POPULATION - STEPFAMILIES

Life went on. I left the Program and had to decide how I was to continue my career. My options included moving up into the state hierarchy. It was a distinct possibility, because I was the first nonpsychiatrist in the State of Maryland to be appointed to head a mental health unit. Because of my role in the Program, my reception might have been less than ideal but more fundamentally I considered the hierarchy to be venal and inward-turning if not just plain dysfunctional. Or I could try to move to NIMH, but again I was not impressed. The tide was turning in the country, so it might not have been a good place to be. Instead I sought a private practice option but maintained consultation activities with the Division of Vocational Rehabilitation and a drug program at a large nonprofit psychiatric hospital near Baltimore.

But the biggest force in the years to come was created by my getting a divorce. When I remarried, my new wife and I faced a very rude awakening in regard to our future.

I will never forget the day when we were standing outside our home and talking about our bright future together. I turned around and looked down into the faces of our four small children. My wife's two boys were upset and angry that they were having to move and would not see their father on a daily basis. My two daughters were in my custody for reasons that meant problems for all of us.

My wife and I were propelled into work to develop what would become the Stepfamily Association of America. It was a lifeline for us and led us to work with the leading experts on the issues of stepfamily adjustment. By force of events we became experts ourselves and opened a specialty practice to help stepfamilies.

Out of all these experiences came our book *Stepfamilies: The Step By Step Model of Brief Therapy.* It was the definitive model for intervention with stepfamilies. It paralleled the model I had learned to use in Baltimore so many years before.

Principles as applied to stepfamilies were phrased as assumptions in the book:

Stepfamily Assumption #1:	Stepfamilies are normal families, valuable and viable in their own right.
Inner City Assumption:	Inner city clients are normal individuals suffering stress by virtue of environmental factors and poverty.
Stepfamily Assumption #2:	Developmental processes drive stepfamily adjustment.
Inner City Assumption:	Survival issues and adaptation to a multitude of stressors drive adjustment.

Stepfamily Assumption #3:	The structure of the stepfamily predicts issues that will be a focus of treatment.
Inner City Assumption:	The form, magnitude and type of stressors will guide management and intervention.
Stepfamily Assumption #4:	Expectations and beliefs about how the stepfamily and its members will operate need to be examined and shifted to a more realistic perspective.
Inner City Assumption:	An expectation regarding stability and a reasonable future needs to be established and management tools provided to organize stressors and ameliorate their effects.

The general points were common to stepfamilies and inner city residents and related to normalization and a reality focus. It turned out that stepfamilies were looked at in terms of the basic model and specific approaches were applied.

- Using the inner city model with its reality focus yielded the observation that stress in stepfamilies is normal and expected at the beginning. It must be dealt with however it might be manifested. It need not reflect psychopathology.
- In the inner city, the medical model often proved injurious and for stepfamilies it was often found that prior treatment had all too often been inappropriate and posed a barrier to forming a relationship with a therapist. Stepfamily clients commonly reported inappropriate and unhelpful intervention.
- In common for the inner city population and stepfamilies it was found that the passive, blank screen of psychoanalysis had to be dispensed with. Not only did stepfamily members need a therapeutic and supportive relationship with a "real" person but it was helpful to have a model for success which helped guide clients and gave them hope.
- Both populations had to be deemed in crisis and professional passivity was not indicated. The clients required active rather than passive intervention in that the problems were often environmental, structural, ongoing, and not intrapsychic. Stepfamilies needed information immediately and helpful management suggestions. For example, "You have to make time for your marriage. If you don't have a lock on your bedroom door, get one. And use it."

For both populations the following applied:

- Diagnoses had a role but only with specific classes of problems and how they were manifested.
- The preliminary response was crisis oriented, with people seen as soon as possible and given as much information as possible.
- The initial focus was on assessing and affecting real-life problems.
- There were no rigid formats in the initial interview. It was essential to move on whatever problems were presented even if a thorough history had not been obtained.
- It was effective to organize thoughts using an energy model assuming people had limited energy to deal with a high-problem environment. When problems were resolved and stressors removed, they had more energy to deal with life. In short, "they got better".
- Response to the initial intervention gave guidance for the continuing form of intervention. If the assumption of normalcy and the energy assumptions were correct, then there was a rapid increase in comfort and better functioning. It was an economical approach.

Contact with a stepfamily typically began with a call from a woman expressing distress about herself, a child in her family or her marriage. Once it was apparent that it was a stepfamily, she was requested to bring her husband with her for an initial session. They might insist on bringing a child who was a focus of concern, but the child was not central to the first session.

The first session could typically be divided into four phases.

- Outpouring - The couple would express their distress and focus of concern.
- Family structure - The structure of the family was described and was key to establishing primary issues.
- Evaluation and explanation of issues - Education concerning the issues began along with what the couple could expect especially in regard to their family structure.
- Homework - The focus was on the couple and their working together. If their relationship survived, the family survived. We knew that when it was clear to the children that the new marriage would survive and the old family would not be resurrected, they calmed down and resumed normal development.

If the couple returned the following week reporting improvement, then the assumption of normalcy was validated. The effort of gathering extensive personal histories was avoided. The chances were good that the guidance and information given would mean they would require only periodic sessions.

Similarly, in the inner city, there was an outpouring followed by information gathering regarding the stressors weighing on the client. It was made clear that the clinician would be working in their behalf to aid them with the stressors, and they were given reality-based instructions about how they could manage what was happening in their lives. In common with stepfamily members, the rapid improvement in our inner city clients also validated the assumption of normalcy, and success in affecting stressors meant that only periodic sessions might be required. (For more details about the stepfamily intervention, the reader is directed to the book *Stepfamilies: The Step By Step Model of Brief Therapy.* A few copies are still available at Amazon. We will shortly be publishing a revised edition for Amazon/Kindle readers and it will be available as a PC download as well. Eventually it will also be available for the Sony Reader and Barnes and Noble Nook.)

ANOTHER POPULATION - VETERANS

Slowly we are once again facing the same problem we had to face after World War II - that we do not bring people back from war, muster them out and expect them to live happily ever after.

I first came face-to-face with the pervasive effects of war when I was working with a man who had mystifying symptoms and we were getting nowhere in therapy. Finally he had a flash of insight and said simply, "You need to speak to my father."

Next session he brought his father, who had been a bomber pilot on both Ploesti raids against Romanian oil fields in World War II. His father said they lost 90% of their number in each raid; he had survivor guilt because he lived through both while his comrades died. He passed it on to his son.

I had a similar experience with a young Jewish woman who suffered odd symptoms that her history did not explain until she brought in her mother, who had survived the Holocaust.

After World War II our nation was forced to recognize the lasting effect of combat experience and had to assess the adequacy of our response. *The Greatest Generation Comes Home* by Michael Gambone offers invaluable information and perspectives. He makes a number of points that are applicable today. The task of rising to the needs of our returning veterans requires that we as a nation make a significant commitment.

Gambone's important book graphically reveals failures and successes. We succeeded spectacularly in educating a generation but in the end often failed veterans. Then as now, "fiscal conservatives" fought to cut funding and government help for veterans. It seems history is repeating itself in that support for resources to aid veterans is often meager at best.

If we will listen, the stories of the effects of war are all around us. Recently a new friend who was a Vietnam veteran began to express frustration about his experience with his physical health treatment at a Veterans Administration Hospital. When he learned I was a psychologist his story took a marked turn.

He considered that he had Post Traumatic Stress Disorder (PTSD) and confided that he had reached this conclusion on his own years after the end of his combat experience. He had never been evaluated for PTSD until recently, when he mentioned his symptoms at the VA. He felt that he had learned to manage his symptoms and did not want his adjustment tampered with. He had been given no guidance previously and now felt pressured to open an issue he felt he had successfully controlled on his own for twenty plus years. Understandably, now, years later, he wondered what "tampering" with his adjustment would do to him or for him. I could not invalidate his fear.

Over time we took to joking about it. We came to a pragmatic conclusion: "There has to be something wrong with you if you don't have a reaction to being in combat -people were trying to kill you". It was a joke but one with a very serious and realistic message.

His story led me to seek more information. The media were conveying stories about people returning from two wars and we were hearing of high suicide rates and broad issues of PTSD. I chose to talk to a friend who was a retired general. What he told me was chilling.

He said that for the treatment of veterans the country was divided into regions and not all treatments or policies were alike. But his perception was that there were many common problems. It should be emphasized that this officer was committed to his service and distressed by what he saw. We discussed the issues over lunch and he chose an out of the way table so we could talk without being overheard. It was obvious he was sharing something painful. He needed to talk but felt he could not do it publicly.

He referred to the Veterans Administration (VA) as being what he called a "push-pull system". Returning combat veterans had all of their records assembled as they mustered out. At that time they could be advised of benefits and given rec-ommendations. Routinely nothing was said. He said the VA never pushed services. It was up to the veteran to pull the services out of them. They had to ferret out in-formation on services they needed and then advocate for themselves. This kind of behavior was expected of people who were conditioned to taking orders.

With all the public statements about our heroes, one would think we would ac-tively work to see to it that they got everything they needed. But they are routinely denied information. It happened after World War II and it is happening again.

One of the most alarming things I learned from the general concerned PTSD. He said he was clear that the rate of incidence increases over decades and research supports the fact. He noted obvious symptoms of PTSD among his peers as they reached their sixties. It did not go away. In many instances it got worse.

From what I heard, there is a need for a broad reexamination of policy and com-mitment. And the reexamination is not solely the responsibility of the government and the Veterans Administration. We the people need to examine our attitudes and the attitudes of our political representatives.

The broad issue relates to how we, as a society, respond in behalf of our fight-ing men and women in preventive ways and when they become veterans. Again, Caplan's principles and thoughts about prevention at varying levels are germane.

Primary prevention in this instance means not going to war at all and engaging in policies that will productively avoid going to war. We can only hope for wise leaders who will act in our interests.

Secondary prevention comes clearly into focus in the mental health field. It would involve early identification and ensuring ways for early intervention and support. It would involve reframing our view of PTSD and, as much as possible, "normalizing" reactions to the stress of war.

It is then only a short step to tertiary prevention, which would involve combat-ing prejudice against veterans suffering reactions to experiences of combat and in foreign cultures. Again normalization comes into play as views are shaped related to stress rather than fearful perceptions of mental illness.

Additionally, reframing of the view veterans hold of themselves would be help-ful. A tightly knit group with a firm commitment to mutual well-being is essential in a combat unit but can have negative effects when it comes to reentering the larger society. Closed ranks as a process after service deserves rethinking. Rethinking suggests that it would be well to have people who represent the larger society (vol-unteers) make contact with veterans and their families at the time of mustering out.

Then it becomes a matter of friendly neighbors who represent the larger society welcoming them home and providing information and support.

Some things we could consider are:

- Shortly after mustering out, each veteran could be contacted by a volunteer. No need for a new huge bureaucracy.
- Trained volunteers would hand out and discuss information concerning benefits and services and where to get them.
- The volunteers would not be responsible for doing crisis intervention and would be instructed to give information about options if there is a major crisis.
- We are seeing a large and steadily increasing population of retired people, and among them are mental health professionals. They would make ideal volunteers because they might be able to identify problems. They would use their skills to get a view of need and give information on resources while maintaining appropriate "distance".
- In the inner city, one issue we dealt with was the contention that Black people should be seen by Blacks and White people by Whites. We found it unnecessary - and I believe the same can be said for the contention that the visits to veterans should only be made by veterans. We are not trying to send people in to close ranks but to make contact in the interest of the veteran, his or her family and our society. It is not time to share war stories but to open up relationships as the veterans return to the larger society and are educated about resources. All of us need to share the burdens.
- Ideally the contact would be at home, with the spouse or family and the veteran. Making contact with a spouse could be crucial as the person who might best identify problems early and help in overcoming denial. Family members would be aware of a lifeline to which they could turn. This process harkens back to the established view in the inner city that a focus on the family was often essential.
- As a matter of policy, we might want to change our term from *posttraumatic stress disorder to posttraumatic stress reaction*. The change of terminology is a normalization piece, because what may happen has a high degree of probability of happening and avoids labeling the veteran as pathological. If people seek help early, concerning a common reaction, it reshapes the process entirely.
- Normalization and early intervention with availability of information would serve a preventive purpose. Conveying the view that a reaction to combat is normal would be crucial.

- It would also be useful to take a hard look at rehabilitation procedures. As a person who suffered a catastrophic auto accident and underwent six years of recovery, I was shocked by how routine the procedures were. My wife and I insisted on taking them over ourselves. Putting ourselves in charge had a much better result and also meant significantly lower costs. It would be well to take a close look at how much veterans can be empowered by changes in the approach to rehabilitation.

The general points are:

- Just as in the inner city, intervention would focus on normalization and dealing with understandable life processes.
- The reaction of people to high stress is generally predictable and should not be considered pathological.
- A ponderous bureaucratic system staffed exclusively by expensive, highly trained workers is not necessary. There are a number of options including community workers, visiting nurses who can be eyes and ears regarding need, or even some form of volunteer corps specific for the purpose from all age groups. Of course, in an aging population with a long life expectancy, we could surely mobilize a cadre of volunteers.
- Early intervention with information and understanding serves a preventive function.
- The problems are ones we face together as citizens of this country and need not be hidden nor stigmatized.

ANOTHER VIEW - LOOKING FOR TALENT NOT DEFICIENCIES

The medical model has an unintended consequence. It reinforces the tendency to look for deficiencies and pathology. In the area of psychology it tends to cause us to overlook patterns of talent.

Over the years I did a lot of psychological testing with both children and adults. The results forced me to look carefully at what I had learned in my training.

For example, I was taught that normal intelligence should show reasonable consistency in the scores of subtests across such tests as the Wechslers. In testing I often found large discrepancies. When the WISC still had Verbal and Performance scores, it was not uncommon for some children to show lower subtest scores on the Verbal section of the WISC. To assume that it reflected a learning disability seemed questionable. Interestingly these children often came from working-class families where Performance abilities were crucial for the types of jobs their parents performed. I found it more instructive to look for patterns of talent rather than deficiencies.

In one instance I tested an eight year old girl who had unmeasurably high Performance abilities while barely making it into the "bright normal" range verbally. As measured, the verbal/performance discrepancy exceeded 30 points often interpreted as indicative of a learning disability. Was this a deficiency or a pattern of talent? She went on to be a very successful film editor.

In short, it is useful to step back away from the medical model which implies pathology. When we do, we may see patterns of relative talent and once again redefine what is normal. It may not be typical, but it may be normal for that person, that family, or that environment and, viewed properly, might highlight personal talent and resources.

NORMALIZATION FOR INTERVENTION

Interventions in these ways and with these populations have much in common. One thing is clear, these types of interventions avoid serous problems associated with using the medical model. With an economy of service, the people involved are viewed as having normal, understandable reactions where intervention and perspective can lighten their burdens, prevent deterioration of functioning and help us work together in a broader societal context. If the assumption is wrong, it will become apparent and we can change our approach.

Chapter 9
Unhealthy Health Politics

CONTEXT

Some sections of this book present an ideal of what should be possible for a community mental health program to achieve in the inner city. Other parts present my conclusions based on my experience in a growing program. Errors made by the staff and administration have been discussed, but the politics have not been given sufficient attention.

Politics requires separate treatment because it represented an omnipresent problem. In referring to politics I am not referring to interference from elected officials, because they were generally not a problem. In some situations failures to solve problems led to public strife, but even then the elected officials rarely intervened in an important way. Rather, the politics to which I refer are those which took place within the hierarchy of mental health personnel.

THE OAK GROVE DEBACLE

Oak Grove, as it shall be called, was a small community of about 14,000 people in far south Baltimore. It was predominantly Black and was dominated by a large public housing project which had been built over thirty years before. Because of its relatively isolated geographical position, it had a history of being bypassed by health and mental health services and the people in the community correctly felt they needed additional services.

The Program opened the Southern Satellite facility in the Oak Grove community of Baltimore in the fall of 1970. The area was not included in the original catchment area specified in the federal staffing grant. Opening the satellite created problems regarding federal matching funds and the planning of the Program.

Although the community did have numerous problems, including a high crime rate and considerable drug traffic, it received an unduly negative reputation as the result of publicity attendant to the placement of the Program's facility.

Oak Grove needed increased services but, in terms of future Program expansion, it was only a small portion of a larger area that was ultimately to be served. The larger area included a number of communities that differed substantially in their racial and class composition. Some of them were very small, isolated communities that were as impoverished as any area of the city (White or Black) and one of them was a large middle-class White community. The people of these other communities, no matter what their race, did not desire to enter Oak Grove, which was, in fact, out of their way. Thus, the total area represented a challenge to planning in order to provide services for such a diverse population. It seemed, however, that there were some neutral areas that might have been appropriate locations for mental health clinics with some hope of serving a broad range of the population.

As noted, it was not planned to provide services until a much later program expansion and opening the area to services raised serious questions about sources of funds and the agreement relating to the current staffing grant. However, the Oak Grove community, or at least some people who considered themselves spokesmen for the community, were viewed as one constituency of a major mental health official.

There was also a group of drug addicts who had banded together in a self-help program and received a great deal of publicity about their claims for overwhelming drug problems in Oak Grove. The claims were vastly inflated but they were accepted at face value by mental health officials, possibly because the claims served mutual purposes. These two pressure groups joined forces with mental health officials, and a meeting was called with top administrative officials from the Program. Arriving at the meeting, the administrative staff learned that it was not really to be a discussion but it was a high pressure operation to force a decision to open a facility in Oak Grove immediately. Unwittingly, the news media, by providing television news cameras, helped increase the pressure. Saying no to the demands at that juncture would have been difficult for the administrators but not altogether impossible and the consequences would have been rather insignificant in comparison with what ensued.

It was finally determined that a trailer would be located in a church parking lot in the area and that the new satellite would operate temporarily in these obviously inadequate quarters. Money for the new endeavor was not in the current budget, and time dragged on amid growing community furor while high-level health officials vacillated and repeatedly failed to make definitive decisions. The Program was cast as the villain and health officials were skillful in continuing to blame the Program for the delays. Months dragged by with no trailer, no staff, and continuing exploitation of the situation by competing groups attempting to strengthen their power position. Visits were made by city and state officials who came to view this "tragic" community, which was becoming publicized as the most dangerous in the city in terms of drug abuse and crime. In fact, it was no worse than many other city neighborhoods.

Even the form of the program and its staffing could not be decided upon. If it was to be managed by the larger program, it was supposed to be a comprehensive outpatient clinic, but community pressure fueled from various sources created interest in having a drug program. It became increasingly clear that there were not enough addicts in the area to justify a full-fledged drug treatment program and that it would be inequitable, given that many other sections of the city had no services at all for drug addicts. In addition, it seemed that some sources, including at least one church, were developing resistance to a broadly conceived mental health clinic because it might include activities such as making referrals for abortions.

Finally, a trailer was installed and services begun. The perception of the community as to who was creating the problem and why such delays existed was gradually changing and the initial staff of the clinic found themselves reasonably well received. Even then, however, there was a belated awareness that the choice of location might be unfortunate and talk was beginning about another site for the facility. This discussion came rather late because the community was already smarting under the onus of an unjustified reputation, politics indicated it was too late for effective planning, funds had been expended, and a great deal of costly professional time had been consumed. The period of this conflict and the indecision was months in duration and damaging to all involved.

If state officials had genuinely desired to serve this area and were willing to bear the cost without matching federal funds, then they should have most properly consulted the Program and indicated their willingness to proceed on that basis. Then, a fast but good objective study could have been undertaken to assure high-quality services in the appropriate location without attendant damaging publicity. The desire of some officials to enhance their reputation with a constituent group took precedence over responsible action and the leadership of the Program was unwilling to make an initial stand, which would have prevented the ensuing debacle.

Fortunately, events eventually turned in favor of Oak Grove. When a permanent facility was proposed for the satellite, other agencies expressed interest in providing services for the area and a multipurpose center came into existence. Now groups in the community banded together to improve the image of the community. Thus, in spite of an unfortunate series of incidents and behavior of public officials that made the situation unnecessarily volatile and damaging, the people of Oak Grove had at last come together and seemed relatively pleased with the services available to them.

This story was all too typical for that time. It was tumultuous, and public officials often were at odds with reality while "community" leaders of questionable leadership qualities played the stage for all they could get. In many ways we were proud concerning our advisory board because we had avoided this kind of circus.

PUBLIC HEARINGS

Often it is apparent that public hearings are neither hearings nor truly public. Rather, they represent an opportunity for power groups to vie for position, gain publicity, and form alliances under the banner of democratic participation in decision making. Such was the experience of the Program with the public hearings held in regard to the planned construction of the central building for the Program.

It was a rather peaceful Monday morning when I came to work and found a message to call the central office. The personnel in the central office knew little except that it had been announced by the new official heading mental health for the State that planning for the central building had been ordered stopped. The public statement from the official's office about cessation of planning included statements that appeared to indicate that the "community" did not want the building and that the money might be needed for comprehensive health centers in other sections of the city.

With each new "clarification" the story was changed slightly but, the basic themes seemed to relate to a desire to utilize the funds for other projects. Information obtained later suggested that the impetus for this decision came from a group of private physicians who had an investment in utilizing the funds for their own purposes. Their concerns were unrelated to the well-being of the community at large, and certainly they were not speaking for the community served by the Program. These facts were learned only belatedly and it was necessary to respond to the initial threat even though there was little hard information to go on. The newly formed advisory board was instantly solidified by this event.

Definitive information was slow in coming, but a commitment was made by state officials to hold public hearings, locations unspecified, about the future of the building. There was a continuing refusal by these officials to clarify intent or procedures to Program personnel, and requests by the advisory board for information led to no meaningful response. The board and the Program staff wished first of all to know where the hearings would be held, fearing that officialdom would use the old trick of holding poorly advertised hearings in some obscure section of the city. In the meantime letters of support from other agencies were obtained and the staff alerted key members of the community to the situation as it was currently understood.

It should be noted that the staff was not wholly in favor of the building as originally conceived and would have welcomed a benevolent reconsideration of the plan which might have led to a considerably less expensive structure. Thus, if it had been done properly, it might have been possible to redesign the building to make it more economical and more suitable for the Program, and there most likely would have been money left for other needed health facilities to be located elsewhere. However, the actions taken by the health hierarchy dictated an all-or-nothing defense.

When the advisory board received no acceptable answers to their written and telephoned inquiries, they removed themselves directly to the state offices and demanded a hearing. They had announced their intentions by a registered letter and had proof of receipt by the State. Nevertheless, when the board arrived at the state offices, the officials denied any foreknowledge of their visit. But through this kind of pressure, information was finally obtained from the State about hearings which were to be well advertised and held in largely appropriate locations in the catchment area - with one exception. One location for the hearings was outside what was then the catchment area, and it became clear that the health officials themselves had not even researched the matter sufficiently to know the Program boundaries. Further, the publicity in the area outside the catchment area was so vague that people came expecting to talk about comprehensive health programs.

The hearings which I attended were largely a travesty. The representatives of the State sitting as the investigative committee were confronted by a hostile gathering of community people and program staff. Some staff breached the bounds of acceptable public statements which could be made by public employees. The citizenry and advisory board members often prevented the committee members from speaking. It became a shouting match with ludicrous overtones that would echo later in the town hall debates about health care reform in 2009. As a counterpoint to the angry exchanges, representatives of numerous groups appeared to deliver statements about wholly unrelated mental health issues, and many of these groups not only did not relate to the inner city but were clearly using the hearings for their own purposes, knew nothing about the problem, and were engaging in public relations activities.

It was in the early days of Muslim conversions in the Black community. In marched a single file of men wearing fezzes and proclaiming their loyalty to Islam. Each community group seemed to have its own agenda. The meeting became a cacophonous gathering observed by bemused "investigative" officials and competing media. The head of the State's Department of Health and Mental Hygiene came in and sat down next to me, expecting to anonymously observe the "hearings". I changed my seat for "greater personal safety".

Serious errors were made by the health officials. The initial information to which they responded evidently came from a group that could not speak for the community to which the Program related. Apparently the statements of this group were not investigated, and impulsive, ill-conceived action was taken. It was also incredible that in that day public officials had not yet understood the roll of the media and that they thought they could expect to make such a move in the inner city and not meet considerable opposition.

Our staff had spent years organizing in the area. There was discontent about the building, but no reasonable redesign could have been entertained in the hostile environment generated. It was also evident that the public officials had little substantive knowledge about the Program, and during the hearings information had to be supplied to them by the advisory board members - information that the state officials should have already possessed and could have obtained easily. The state officials conveyed the impression that they were so sure of themselves that they could make unilateral decisions without fear of consequences.

In the end an embarrassed administration decided that the planning for the building would continue. The hearings and the events surrounding them served one largely negative function. It increased the hard feelings between the Program and state officials. It also demonstrated the latter entity's abysmal ignorance concerning a program they were supposedly administering.

It had some positive effects, however. It served to consolidate the advisory board, made public officials more judicious in their decisions regarding the

Program, furthered the education of the community to the purposes of the Program, permitted staff to meet new community groups, and brought support from the State for jobs for community people.

The hearings represented a failure of cooperative ventures, failure of planning, official pettiness, inability to research background information, improper perception of power groups, a misreading of public sentiment, misperception of the extent of the power of state officials, and the dangers in power politics among state officials as contrasted to responsible action to meet the needs of the public.

In fact, the failure of officials to make desirable changes was more damaging to their image than an open admission that circumstances had changed and new data were available. Even under the prevailing political climate, changes could have been made without a public statement of any kind and could have been based upon an agreement among interested professionals in the Program, the State, the University, and community representatives. The unwillingness of officials to redesign the central building earlier was a factor in the unfortunate public hearings.

It was, in short, an excellent example of how not to perform duties and demonstrated clearly that it cannot be assumed that health personnel share common purposes. Handled differently, the state officials might well have gotten at least part of what they wanted for the greater benefit of all involved.

POLITICS AMONG PROFESSIONALS

And then there was the matter of politics among mental health professionals who were supposedly above it all but where it was an omnipresent problem. Our young staff was naive about politics at the beginning but had to learn quickly about a number of ways politics was manifested.

- Power, prestige and money - Advancement, power, prestige, and money depended upon political alliances within and among the professions, and, thus, politics became more of an issue than doing the best possible job of designing and delivering services. Although community mental health was a service field, it frequently was cast into an arena of interests which represented self-service as empires declined and rose and potential sources of funds both personal and programmatic had direct or indirect effects on the future and fortunes of programs.
- Constituencies - The facts were that mental health officials had constituencies, and their promises to them led to considerable pressure in regard to the location

of a facility and the form and orientation of the Program. In one of the cited instances, because of politics, a selected site was wholly undesirable and made it difficult to deliver services. For the mental health official, delivering a service now might be considerably more important politically than delivering well-planned services for a larger group that would also benefit the smaller group of constituents. Thus, gathering data and information on a community came to relate at least in part to a defense against politically inspired pressure and the force of constituencies.

- Guarding Turf - The suspiciousness that existed among programs and components of the mental health system was often a function of health politics and related turf issues. Desired control of facilities by highly placed officials and the attendant status and increased financial reward frequently led to the creation of a climate of suspicion.
- Inflexibility - Programmatic dysfunctions were further increased by the actions of officials who felt they were unable to change plans on the basis of newly acquired data. New data and new experiences might require a change in plans, but an unwillingness to change plans either represented shortsightedness and inflexibility or indicated that officials feared that changes would make them politically vulnerable. In part, health officials relating to the Program acted as if they could not change the concept of the proposed central building because it somehow reflected negatively on their abilities as planners.

And then there were cardinal principles senior staff had to keep in mind in order to effectively deal with politics.

- Defense - Working for the development of a program included the necessity to be prepared for political gamesmanship and the clear recognition that a program may not be permitted to grow in the most logical fashion on a sound base of planning. The administration had to be willing at key points to make definitive stands about the design and service elements of a program in order to help counter the effects of various forms of political intrigue. These stands might have been temporarily unpopular but the longer-term effect had to be considered.
- Premature Promises - Because of politics in the mental health hierarchy and in the community, the administration and staff needed to be alert to the negative consequences of making premature and ill-advised promises under pressure. Impulsively making promises is an understandable mistake, because there is

sufficient pressure in merely managing a program without having to deal with armies of discontented constituents of mental health officials. Once promises were made, they tended to lead to a spiral of promises to every competing group, which could not possibly be fulfilled. It was obviously a shortsighted method of managing outside politically induced pressure, and sooner or later the recipients of the promises came to cash their checks.

- Anticipating Politics - Another major point related to the very basics of planning. Planning involves much more than gathering data on specific needs and developing a service which meets those needs. Planning and day-to-day administration include anticipation of probable political effects and opposition.

THE PUBLIC LOSES

The existence of power politics in the mental health field is endemic and reveals the degree to which "public servants" are capable of merely serving themselves and their constituencies. Health politics may theoretically serve positive functions in facilitating checks on the power of elected officials and may foster the expression of views of portions of the community. However, the purposes of mental health professionals may be similar to the worst purposes of elected officials when they seek to elevate their status and power and increase financial rewards. When these matters are the primary motivating forces, then effective planning and service delivery are subordinated and the public good is in no way served.

Roger B. Burt

Chapter 10
Was Community Mental Health a Failure?

CONTEXT

Community mental health was a bold experiment that in all likelihood was doomed to fail from the beginning. The problems militating against success were both local and national. At the local level in Baltimore the Program was not well supported by either of the supervising entities, the University and the State. These problems were surely replicated in programs across the country. At the national level, the end of the reform movement and various political and economic realities combined to defeat its objectives.

Was it all a waste and merely a doomed experiment? Perhaps not. The "laboratory" to test new ideas was not evaluated, but important lessons were learned. The knowledge gained can still be used. And now that a new reform movement is beginning, could we be looking at an opportunity for a new chapter in the delivery of mental health services?

Offering mental health services in the inner city was challenging, especially because neither training nor the literature gave sufficient reality-based guidance or direction. A program which was meant to be a laboratory for service delivery was never evaluated and was viewed as a troublesome and annoying source of funding. In essence, a young, dedicated but inexperienced staff had to develop their own viable service model and provide those services virtually without support or guidance.

The staff of the Program found ways to be of substantial help to the inner city residents, ways to relate to the community by involving representatives in the Program, ways to effectively employ community residents, and ways to relate to community agencies through effective service lures. But building an effective organization led

149

to the recognition of some basic issues that went beyond simply developing the best possible services.

HARSH REALITIES AND CONFLICTING INTERESTS - LOCAL FACTORS

Chapter 2 outlined the heritage of the poor and major components of the heritage of professionals and showed how these problems had to be overcome to provide a meaningful and effective service delivery system. Heritage was viewed as something considerably more than a matter of history. Heritage was alive with effects that were woven into the fabric of both the moment and the context. Heritage is a part of the culture that people carry. Once understood and recognized, the heritage of an individual helps reveal the origins of current problems and what supports them by factors not based in psychopathology.

Those of us who believed in total management took a broad-based approach in working with clients. We knew they had often found systems unresponsive and would view us with suspicion. At the same time we had to make hard choices in terms of allocating time and effort.

In addition, clinicians found themselves confronted at every turn with the most basic kinds of discrimination. Racism can be managed but probably will never disappear from service agencies. Composition of staff, design of services, and orientation toward specific client groups may all be a function of racism.

In most cases there was even less recognition of the insidious influence of classism. The simple fact was that White inner city residents did not get any better service than Black inner city residents. It could be said that the business of the poor was just not wanted.

And then there was the matter of administration and who held the purse strings. The staff of the Program had to confront these issues from two controlling entities.

As to the University, the first question was why they even wanted to have any responsibility for what the grant said was a service-oriented program. The answer almost surely lay in the two words "money" and "training".

We saw instances of money initially being used to hire people who did not actually work in the Program. The amount of misdirected funds was not huge, but it indicated that there was an orientation to use the funds to support existing services.

Tuition and fees from charges to patients did not supply anywhere near the funds necessary for the maintenance of the medical school programs. Building expansion and staff salaries often came by way of grants for research, training, or service projects. At times some of these funds might not be applied to the specific projects for which they were obtained. But any source of funding was of interest.

As to training, early on it became clear to us that the University wanted to move medical students and residents into the program for training purposes. The firm opposition of the staff prevented it. And the service model of the type designed for total management did not mesh well with programs oriented toward the finer points of treating psychopathology using the medical model.

No doubt, for the University, another benefit was status. Community mental health was a new and trendy movement and hosting such a program enhanced status. Being able to cite the existence of a new type of program was a means for attracting medical students and psychiatric residents. And, as already noted, it looked good on the curriculum vitae of the academic staff to be able to indicate that they consulted with a community mental health program. They also had the opportunity to write "timely" articles. They soon learned that the headache of having to deal with an unruly staff and a difficult city environment outweighed status.

The State, on the other hand, was more service-oriented but also viewed the Program as a source of funds. We couldn't help wondering why they thought a short-term grant would yield the State much of value in terms of its own long-term funding.

Again, as with the University, there seemed to be considerable "fuzzy" thinking. The program might have been an opportunity to integrate existing systems that would have been mutually beneficial, but turf wars and jealously guarded funding held sway. They showed no vision and never undertook a valuable opportunity to do an evaluation and learn from their "laboratory".

There was a significant opportunity to get funding from the federal government for a central building. The hearings outlined earlier were largely about defending the funds for the original purpose, while State officials tried to divert the funds for other purposes. The staff developed very negative views of the University and the State, and they both gave us a great deal to complain about. Many of the problems could have been overcome or mitigated if there had been a real dedication to an evaluation process from which all parties could have learned.

In regard to the University, using a community mental health grant for physical expansion, attracting students, and fostering interaction between academic and service staff did not constitute a major problem in and of itself. In most cases, a university medical school can openly state its reason for desiring a community mental health program and offend virtually no one.

The problems arose on the operational service end of the relationship. Community mental health personnel and academic personnel had two very different charges and orientations. The charges need not be exclusive in theory or even in practice. Excellent training can be obtained by giving the best possible services -unless, of course, the training was oriented toward a vastly different kind of practice. It was in practice that conflict arose.

When the Program was under the control of the University, there was tremendous conflict. The University was supposedly joining the reform movement, but in doing so the University personnel seemed to the staff to have no desire to change their modes of operation. My stance was quite simple. Our foremost goal was to be effective, and we would not perpetuate exploitation of our population in the interest of training. Granted, everyone must begin his or her career with someone, but circumstances are crucial determinants of who that someone should be. Training had to adapt to the reality of needed service. It is not good training if it does not reflect the realities of the requirements of the service environment and population.

In contrast, social work students were placed for an entire year with a supervisor on-site and made a valuable contribution. But medical students coming for six weeks were superfluous to Program needs and damaging to the clients. Further, they were kept separate and supervised by people who often had never had any experience providing services for or meeting the needs of inner city residents. In short, the social work students demonstrated that training and service could be combined to the benefit of everyone, but the medical personnel in the setting were unwilling to alter their training model.

If the medical faculty had changed approaches and, for example, moved toward the family treatment model developing at the time, whereby students would begin following families for the duration of their training and concerned themselves with physical and mental health, there would have been a substantial change in the willingness of the staff to cooperate. However, the staff was strongly against perpetuating the service abuses that had been so evident and which had contributed to the problems of the people they were seeing.

On a continuing basis the staff had to face the hostility of medical personnel who questioned their competence, were unwilling to seek a compromise, and seemed bent on continuing to operate from an inflexible and classist perspective. Staff unrest about this situation was a major contributor to the administration of the Program being given over to the State.

It should be emphasized that the staff were ambivalent about the change because the State officials had not indicated any real interest in the Program, either. Staff questioned the State's motives, realizing that state officials had their own constituencies and personal agendas related to power, money, and status. Yet it seemed the lesser of two evils. Being administered by the State had, on the whole, been beneficial, at least in terms of permitting the continuation of services most responsive to the needs of the inner city residents. The experience of the Program demonstrated that, while on paper the reasons for an alliance between a community mental health program and a university may sound good, the problems were harsh and burdensome in the area of operations. It seemed best to be controlled by public agencies in which service considerations for this type of population had a high priority.

FAILINGS OF PROFESSIONALS

Our experience in this Program showed many failings that probably appeared in other programs.

- New programs often attracted grandiose leaders, with sometimes seriously damaging effects.
- Clinical and administrative interests were not reconciled.
- Competition among professions did not lead to a common cause.
- Attention to budget building took precedence over learning to provide effective service.
- The evolution of staff from groundbreakers to managers was not fostered.
- There was a failure to balance top-down and bottom-up experience - no internal partnership.
- There was a failure to relate to and develop community resources on an ongoing, effective basis.
- Excessive idealism did not sustain reality-based programs.
- Effective evaluations either specific or conceptual, were not undertaken.
- There was no such thing as an exit interview

The decline of community mental health was a national phenomenon, but the problems seen in the Baltimore program were surely fairly typical of local issues.

Some of the most valuable lessons come from negative experiences. The simple list above gives guidelines to consider for the development of a successful program.

OVERSELLING COMMUNITY MENTAL HEALTH - CONCEPT VERSUS REALITY

Enthusiasm for this new endeavor was marvelous to behold, and the staff of the Program was infected by it. It was clearly long overdue for the mental health systems to redirect their efforts and try new approaches. Academic and service personnel banded together in the search for national recognition of needs. The conclusions of these people, in their intent to broaden the availability and responsiveness of service systems, cannot, in the main, be faulted.

However, community mental health was seriously oversold. The forces of the decade of the 1950s that culminated in the community mental health movement and the poverty programs characterized an era in which professionals expected to have more impact than was possible. The concepts were sound, but there was a fundamental problem in the setting of attainable goals and, even more basically, a failure of vision.

The writings of Gerald Caplan were timely in applying the public health model and correct in pointing out larger forces that affected the mental health of the population as a whole. The writings of Caplan indicate that he had an excellent grasp of the principles, and his work is well worth studying. The problems came in the day-to-day reality of implementation. Also, practice demonstrated, at least in the inner city, that the tasks related to prevention were often much beyond the ability of the individual practitioners and also beyond the kind of programs designed.

As indicated in this book, community mental health in the inner city could do a great deal - much less than was hoped, but a great deal nonetheless. Unrealistic promises and visions of a comprehensive national network of programs as part of the War on Poverty yielded a good flow of initial funding which could not be sustained. Moreover, the political climate of the country was about to change.

A HARD BLOW AND A HARD RIGHT - THE NATIONAL CONTEXT

Not only was the political climate of the country about to change but so too was the climate of reform itself.

The Poverty Program promised a great deal, and in the end the poor found once again that the benefits disappeared because of political shifts and entrenched interests. During the War on Poverty, programs came and went, each with its own fanfare. And as the fanfare faded there was a corresponding death of belief and hope, which bred ever-increasing cynicism and hardened resistance. But worse was to come.

The day Dr. King was assassinated was a crucial day for America. Our staff went into shock, but we all weathered the riots and the storm among ourselves. What we could not know at the time was the long-term effect on the area we served.

Slowly I began to perceive a loosening of the ties between the Black community and the dedicated workers who had come to help. We had been welcomed, but now there was increasing suspicion and it felt as though the welcome mat had been taken in.

Looking back at other aspects of the situation, I believe I could detect a shift within the Black community, dividing the people who were still dedicated to grasping the next rung on the ladder from those who walked away from the ladder in disgust. Gains were made for some people who worked toward an entry into the middle class and succeeded. Some other people assumed an attitude that ensured they would remain in the "left behind". I cannot document these changes but that is how it felt.

At the same time the political pendulum was swinging. The post-World War II reform movement was ending. The joys of sex, drugs and rock 'n' roll became the fight for abortion rights, the struggle with addictions and ambivalence about disco.

We became preoccupied with Nixon, Watergate and then the "Conservative Revolution" was upon us as a reassuring actor moved into the White House.

The funds for noble initiatives dried up and the commitment to community mental health with it. It didn't matter anymore if the movement had been oversold. It would not be funded. Commitments were elsewhere. The dark side of many conservatives showed a callous attitude toward the poor and disadvantaged. Christian charity seemed to have been abandoned.

If professionals and poverty workers were vacillating and groping for effective programs, their uncertainty could at least be excused. But then the retrenchment became more serious and more damaging because it was at the national level and the poor could see that in the end very little had changed for them. The bright hope seemed to be over, and seems again to be a glimmer in our current economic environment. But did we come out with nothing?

Sometimes it isn't a matter of winning the war, because it may not have been a war that could have been won. Often it is better to ask how well we did and whether we learned anything.

Mental health professionals had a great deal to be proud of in that they found ways to make functional commitments to work on the problems of the mental health of the poor. While facing the mental health problems and finding ways to serve the poor, they had also tried to face up to issues of both poverty and discrimination. Of course, not everyone in the field shared commitments to improve our service delivery, and it would be foolish to declare that racism and classism had been overcome.

What affects the outcome of a movement is often hard to define. But we can define three major factors that made negative contributions in this case:

1. System instability and failures
2. Failings of professionals
3. Changes in national policy.

THE LIMITS OF INHERENT ACTIVISM

Whenever there is a reform movement, the lure of activism is considerable. In Baltimore we did not see ourselves as merely doing a job, merely applying our knowledge in a new place. We saw ourselves as activists, and the tendency to be an activist was enhanced by the opposition we felt from the State and the University. The people we were seeing needed help badly and we were there to give it and thereby change the system. But many of our colleagues seemed more interested in preserving their positions, protecting their income, and maintaining perks. We had the vision of youth and they had the vision of the established professional. True change and its continuance required a partnership between the young and the old to channel activism, and such a partnership did not occur.

Our work to involve the community inevitably had an activist element to it. It was tempting and a delicate matter to turn clients into activists even in the interest of their own well-being. Most people simply want to be left alone and to lead a reasonably comfortable life in which they can find happiness and gratification. The vision of armies of the poor demanding and receiving their due is a nice dream but only a dream.Most people don't want to be activists, and the pool of interested and involved people in any community from which to draw effective activists is very small.

Thus, small numbers of people were drawn upon as activists, and the search was on to find the necessary activism to foster continuing reform. In most cases, the staff of a community mental health program looked primarily to their own ranks.

At times, in the climate of reform of those years, more radical activists were willing to attack the system itself regardless of consequences. But underlying the basic duties of a job in an inner city setting and a commitment to the community there was a commitment to the agency and its goals - presumably related to the well-being of the members of the community. Even in the face of agency dysfunction there was a service obligation to be discharged. That obligation might include adjustment of the client to a bad situation when there are no realistic alternatives. Thus, at times some of the work could be quite distasteful, but outrage against inequities could not be gainfully directed too much against the organization itself. We were always doing a delicate balancing act.

CONFRONTING UNEXPECTED ISSUES

In a new endeavor it is almost inevitable that unexpected events will take center stage. The issues may be far larger than something like "mere" ethics and may relate to broad matters of social policy. Some of these matters of concern were well highlighted in an article by Kenneth Keniston in the 1968 July/August Transaction which was entitled "How Community Mental Health Stamped Out the Riots (1968-1978)". It was satire, but there were many real themes mentioned in it made it exceedingly painful reading for individuals who were working in the inner city at the time.

The article was published shortly after the large-scale riots following the assassination of Martin Luther King Jr. It foresaw the possibility of mental health workers becoming a punitive arm of the government and police as well as preventing dissent by the "treatment" of troublesome individuals who were deemed psychopathological.

In fact, at the time of the riots in Baltimore, mental health officials called the clinics of the Program to inquire as to the staff's intentions for helping to control the violence. Staff members were questioned as to whether they were doing anything to control it, and when the answer was negative it was inferred that they were not doing their job.

In advance of the riots, some staff had considered whether it might be possible to intervene with groups at the site of potentially explosive incidents, but when the riots occurred we saw it as purely a police matter. The staff had time to examine their own feelings about the possibility for intervention and decided that it would be of questionable value, because it would jeopardize a somewhat objective position but also because it would implicate the Program as an arm of the power structure that had been "exploiting" the very people who were rioting. Thus, although the staff felt the rioting would serve no useful purpose, they could see neither an appropriate way to intervene nor justification for assuming a control or containment function.

At the time when all services were largely immobilized the staff had the chance to examine their own reactions and racial attitudes. The staff of many other service agencies split along racial lines but, to the credit of the Program staff, they did not segregate themselves but stood as people who were facing a common problem. In the ensuing weeks there was a retrospective analysis of what roles should or could have been assumed, and the staff realized that the pressures to intervene were wholly inappropriate. Thus, the experience confirmed the existence of pressures along the lines of the main theme of the Kenniston article.

Interestingly enough, the riots had a temporary therapeutic value for the client population. Although many people in the inner city were afraid to go out at all, telephone contacts with many clients indicated some fear about the violence but also the appearance of some short-term benefits in the relief of their symptoms.

The rioting took on the character of economic reprisals more than anything else. Crimes against person were not the primary characteristic of the violence. Rather, while it was a riot triggered by an assassination of a beloved and revered leader, the major responses were directed against nearby establishments representing or viewed as representing economic exploitation. It was the property of the "exploiters" and not the exploiters themselves (narrowly or broadly conceived) who were the object of the attacks. To have attempted intervention even in the form of crowd control for the protection of property would have placed mental health personnel clearly on the side of people who were seen as exploiters.

Many times we had to confront not just our place in the system and our role in the community but also our own identity.

BALANCING SERVICE AND SOCIAL CHANGE

Community mental health was unusual in that it was not created for service alone. Activism and change were fundamental if any part of the prevention agenda was to be realized. The art was in balancing the two. It was possible to engage in some social change while employed in a community mental health program, but the limitations were rather severe, partly as a function of responsibility to individuals, partly because of the funding sources, and partly because mental health personnel cannot afford to exaggerate or misestimate the potential for change. More importantly, however, they must consider the possibility, that by providing services to people who are, above all, suffering from direct or indirect effects of such things as classism, racism and an inequitable system, they are participating in their exploitation or perpetuating their misery. By deeming them psychopathological, by "cutting the pain", and by stopgap intervention, the professional may be viewed as merely dampening dissent.

The article by Kenneth Keniston is an exaggerated example of the implicit function that community mental health might have been serving. The casualties were seen as the problem rather than the system that created the casualties.

The above is one stance an activist may adopt, but it is, in the end, an extreme position that only an independent activist may take. Change from within a mental health organization requires a focus on the job which is to be done and the art of the possible within an organization.

Looking back, I see that it was certainly presumptuous of young professionals, many under the age of thirty, to think that they knew more than seasoned senior mental health staff and administrators. But, again, with the wisdom of latter years, it is clear to me that this young staff was not only in tune with the times but, far more dedicated than the entrenched and established professionals. Without intending to, senior professionals drove the staff deeper into the community and voided the possibility of a larger working relationship involving them, the junior staff, and community members. An effective set of partnerships was not possible.

CONCLUSION

It is valid to conclude that a great deal was learned, including the applicability of alternative models of intervention in diverse settings. In places the work continues even if only by tenacious, indigenous people. The experience in Baltimore gave clarity to professional vulnerabilities and systemic failures and it was clear that in the end the climate of the time will surely affect the ideals.

Concepts and ideals do not stand alone when it comes time to implement the elements of a project and reality will prevail. Implicit elements such as inherent activism have to be accounted for and conflicts related to balancing competing interests must be resolved. The entire process will always be more complicated than it was initially assumed and adjustments must be ongoing.

Clearly the potential for the movement was demonstrated but if efforts were to be renewed there would be a need for a more widespread, enduring commitment and partnerships. A renewed effort would not only have to involve using the lessons learned and alternative models but would also require a greater efficiency by employing such people as community workers and volunteers.

If we were to choose to embark on a renewed effort, could we do it better today? And how would we approach the endeavor? Such a challenge is intriguing.

Roger B. Burt

Chapter 11
The Mental Health Challenge Today

THE END OF A NOBLE EXPERIMENT

It is not hard to guess the outcome for the Program or the community workers. A truly workable system of services with a preventive underpinning was developed, but the story clearly indicates that it was not evaluated nor valued by the State or the University.

Federal grant funds ran out two or three years after I left the Program. The initial cadre of dedicated activists who came to the Program moved on. Even before I left I had seen a shift from the hiring of the "can do", adhocratic type of staff to more bureaucratically oriented individuals.

Over time there was a steady retrenchment from the community into the central building, which became more of a fortress rather than a center from which staff reached out to the community. It was decided that consultation and education were not proper activities for a mental health organization and the satellite centers were closed. The medical model again reigned supreme.

Since it was a state system and firing of any kind was not routine, the community workers stayed on, but their ranks were steadily thinned by attrition of various kinds. Replacements were not hired.

"Community" is the important word in describing the movement, and there was always the question whether our society would pick up on a larger commitment beyond traditional services. In the end, locally and nationally, the vision and the spirit of community mental health generally were not supported. The mental health professions and the institutions charged with delivering the services and the guidance all too frequently failed us.

The spirit lives on among individuals within the community who are dedicated to serving their own. Individual efforts supported by small grants tend the flickering flame with vision, compassion, and understanding.

Our vision for the future clearly needs refinement and a firm commitment. As the economy recovers from the recent recession, and we refine our health system, we have the opportunity to define mental health anew and to restate what it means, how we commit ourselves, how we define community, and who the members of our professions want to be.

A MOMENT IN TIME -
A PLACE IN THE BROADER PICTURE OF HISTORY

Community mental health grew out of developments in public policy and views which emphasized prevention and public health initiatives.

Even after the end of the community mental health era, development continued as professionals sought to deal with couples and families and accepted the importance of a societal context. There continued to be some freedom from traditional restraints and the potential for forms of intervention such as those developed in the inner city setting.

Yet public resources devoted to mental health probably reached their high point with the community mental health movement. As the reform movement faded and the conservative era grew, the field faded along with compassion and commitment to all citizens. The conservative movement, by its name, implies an emphasize on preservation but the disinclination of many "conservatives" to support prevention and commitment to community served to foster decline and dysfunction. Too often many of its adherents of conservatism displayed an arrogant self-interest and disdain for being citizens of a community. For a variety of reasons the cohesion and the stability of the mental health movement eroded.

And then something even worse happened. Insurance companies saw a source of profit in the medical field. It was so easy for managed care to save money on mental health treatment. We were ever so vulnerable. Preventive measures were ignored. Everything was run for cost-cutting and profit.

As I look back over the decades of my experience as a psychologist I see both an identity crisis for the field in general and for all the specific mental health professions. But now we are entering a new reform period with dynamic leadership, and it is time to look again at the possibilities.

Dr.King was one of our great leaders back then and a crucial figure in our country's history. He represented so much more than leadership of the civil rights movement and the effect he had on the Black population. His dream was infectious and

162

Roger B. Burt

affected all of us. If not yet fulfilled, it still lives in the minds and hearts of many of us.

Now comes another Black man in a time of reform. It is a second coming of sorts and signals what David Gergen called an "aspirational presidency". A signal has been sent to the world that America now has an immensely talented, thoughtful and intelligent leader. Not just our people but all people can aspire to greater things.

Aspiration takes many forms, and it is also time for the mental health professions to aspire to a reformation.

A PROPOSAL FOR REFORMATION

In Baltimore, so long ago, a small group of dedicated young people looked through a window into a future which might have been and might still be. An underlying public health philosophy directed us to goals which permitted us to break free from the restraints of old roles and selfish interests. We seized an opportunity to strive, to learn, and to build what worked.

Errant guidance or no guidance at all from above forced junior staff to develop their own guidance and direction. So far removed from the gentility of the office of an Austrian physician, we were forced to a new view. Our instructions were taken from the people we served and the circumstances of their lives. We became both teachers and the taught and were equals among ourselves and those around us. We came from differing disciplines with differing talents which could be applied in an adhocratic fashion.

Through that same window, behind the grime, the suffering and the disorder, we glimpsed a pond into which we threw a stone. Over time the ripples moved out and out to show us in so many ways that what we had learned could be applied in other circumstances and had beneficial effects. The ripples did not die out. We can still perceive them and make use of them and the lessons learned.

REFORMING OUR VIEW OF OURSELVES

The elements for the future of "mental health" exist in many forms and thoughts. With our experience and knowledge in the context of another reform movement, it is time to bring them together. Our professions would have to begin with a philosophical evaluation and a conceptual analysis of who we are and what we can and should accomplish.

When the medical model, with its emphasis on disease, is removed as the overarching principle for our professions, it opens the possibility for creating a definition of flexible roles relating to the larger well-being of the members of our society. It seems that the beginning must be to evaluate the meaning and the utility of the term "mental health" itself. It eluded me as a young man and has for me since then only become more elusive. We know the term had utility in moving certain kinds of suffering out of the realm of theology and into a more rational realm where science dwells. But science so often fails in achieving the objectivity it seems to seek and, in itself, does not lead us into the future. We must include it but also look beyond it.

Finding a new term or terms would be helpful and would serve the development of a conceptual framework. From there we would have to move toward detailing what we are and are not to believe is our work. Psychology, for example, is a social science but we wrestle with whether it is either social or a science. Perhaps, in part, it is experimental psychology which is most clearly scientific with the clinical part being more clearly social. *Experimental* can define analysis and evaluation and *social* may lead us to our commitment. But we need broad concepts to begin with and must work for careful definition from there.

Once we have a better view of our role in society we can then move toward specific utilitarian concepts and the knowledge that has been derived from science and research. Utilitarian matters can more clearly come into play as tools and ways to support productive functioning and happiness in our society. Naturally, because our professions are not building and selling concrete objects, we stand to consider charity, empathy and compassion. And in developing a response we consider the impact of culture, war, poverty, family unit form, and so forth. Each of us can choose our particular focus of interest.

Changes in our definition of our professions and ourselves are essential, but, although it is not the focus of a new vision, we have challenges that all people must face. There will always be issues of turf, venality, outdated attitudes and obstructions to vision.

AN ESSENTIAL PROBLEM

The mental health professions have not resolved the problem created by our experience and our body of knowledge. While the body of knowledge grew, we did not redefine who we are and to what we are committed. What we have learned constitutes an essential problem even as it holds out a challenge. It was convenient to create the concept "mental health", then we learned that what we were dealing with was more than physical disease and the medical model was not always a good fit. Unless we resolve the problem, we cannot focus our commitment or the means to make it.

Certainly the disease model, or at least some physical basis for many dysfunctions and suffering, cannot be denied. Psychotic illness with a biochemical basis, organic impairment, disorders related to infectious diseases, the effects of trauma and so on will not disappear from our work no matter how we define them. And, yes, neuroses do exist and are amenable to treatment with drugs and psychotherapy.

But we also need to concern ourselves with management of life transitions (such as noted in stepfamilies), the effects of stress of various kinds (such as coping with a chronically ill child) or quite simply what happens when we become a parent or grow old. Our specialties will have to focus on what must be dealt with physically but then bridge to the functional, spiritual, social, and management issues. In that sense we are a family and must help our family members when they are in distress.

And we need to extend our view beyond what is emergent to what we can prevent not just through intervention but through education and management as well. At times the helping professions have been characterized as having a religious quality. So be it, but there are reality factors and knowledge woven in as well. The essential problem is that our scope has broadened and we need to know how to proceed.

GOALS AND FORMS OF COMMITMENT

Certainly a reexamination of the public health model and preventive possibilities as seen in the writings of people such as Gerald Caplan would be useful. The wellbeing of our society is at stake and it is a luxury to confine our efforts to emergent crises and offer most services to the upper echelons of our society. Again, the words community, charity and compassion come to mind.

Service, social change and prevention all need to be considered. It is difficult to separate them. As noted in the section on activism, there is an eternal need to balance service and activism in behalf of change. Utilitarian concepts have to be meshed with values.

And then there is the matter of how things are approached in the public and the private spheres. How much of what we do is supported by the public and how much is done by private enterprise will forever be an issue. In Baltimore we found that when the State abandoned the community mental health movement it was, in part, taken over by individuals with vision within the community. It is relevant to discuss how they could be supported both publicly and privately.

A good example of a task to be considered is such a thing as our response to the homeless. They are reflective of many things including economic distress and chronic mental illness where circumstances were made worse by the decline of support for public mental hospitals. Also to be considered are the homeless young mothers struggling on the streets with their children.

Some members of our society condemn the homeless and state the belief that they deserve their fate. Such statements are not appropriate from members of a community. But "caring" citizens and professionals have been inattentive as well. How we are to approach these types of issues is still very much open to question. And, I would contend, it should be up to our professions to address these issues publicly and to raise questions regarding values in our society.

ATTENDING TO THE RANGE OF WORKING MODELS

Fundamental to the experience in Baltimore and the lessons learned was the move away from the medical model, which opened a whole range of possible interventions going beyond the individual to community groups and agencies. In fact, intervention with the health care system itself was at issue as well.

While we found there were clearly places for the medical model, it was hardly central to our work. One size did not fit all. Listening to our clients led us to understand that we had to respond to their reality. By normalizing their experiences and intervening in their behalf we instituted an intervention tree. If the initial intervention worked at the level of reality issues, we had saved immense effort and avoided looking for psychopathology. Solving problems and removing stress freed psychic energy, and that led to improved comfort and functioning.

A variant of the same model worked in intervention with stepfamilies and proved economical. Another variant should prove beneficial with veterans, especially if we depathologize PTSD so it becomes PTSR (reaction). Then our target populations become not sick but adapting, and can be open about their distress.

Trying new models is worthwhile in many regards. We never moved tobacco addiction into the mental health realm partly because it was a sanctioned addiction and its use was profitable, not just for tobacco companies but governments as well in terms of taxes. We did, however, identify a public health risk and through education and social sanctions have made steady inroads in decreasing the addiction. And now in Paris even the French are standing on the street outside the cafes smoking. I quit because I was tired of standing alone outside in the cold.

Rather than playing billion-dollar games of cowboys and indians at our borders with drug cartels, we might consider new approaches to drug abuse. Interdiction does not work well, and clearly decreasing demand would be more productive. My time on the streets of Baltimore and as a clinical trainer for the staff of a drug program ("juice" program with methadone) at a major private psychiatric hospital was informative.

The junkies routinely told me that they knew their life on the streets was time limited. Either they got "clean" or they died. Paranoia was normal. Someone really was out to get them, to take either the money they had managed to get for drugs or the drugs themselves. Yet not many got clean the first time. Sometimes when they came for service there were no places for them and so they were turned away and told to return in six months. Every one of us knew what was happening in the interim. Not nearly enough money for treatment was allocated, especially considering the true expense to the public of drug addiction and abuse in general.

To oversimplify, my job as a consultant and clinical trainer was to help sort out the addicts with psychotic or organic illnesses where self-medication may have been at issue, from those who were with the wrong crowd at the wrong time and, for example, may have missed their adolescent adjustment. The means of approach to help them had to be adjusted, but the system was rigid and lacked vision. Some of them badly needed day care for their children and most needed vocational rehabilitation services of one form or another. They might need an education and habilitation services if they never had any job skills at all.

Those are just a few examples of the points to consider in the development of alternative models, which often should include a variety of supportive services tailored to the differing groups of substance abusers. Our educational campaigns and treatment programs stand to be broadened considerably, and drug abuse needs to go out of "fashion".

And then there is the whole matter of how we handle our chronically mentally ill. It is a complex problem, and it may be that doing away with fortress hospitals was not such a bad thing except that we did not replace them with a flexible and humane system. We simply put the people out on the streets. If we aren't going to build a viable system, then we at least need to admit defeat and work to create a compassionate support system, offering them food and comfort in the winter, for example. And in rural areas we need to attend to the homeless huddled in abandoned buildings in the countryside. We can do better than this and sort the economic casualties from the biochemically impaired.

As mentioned, vocational rehabilitation, at least in Maryland, lost its way when it turned to emphasizing services to the severely disabled. Before that there had been funds available to help women coming out of divorce with no marketable job skills because they had been caring for their children their entire adult lives.

Creating a "disability" to permit funding was something of a shell game, but the endeavor was worthwhile. When these women came in the door for services they had the potential to be welfare recipients or employed tax-paying citizens. The choice was an obvious one. The same could be said for many other men and women in the inner city.

Building models also has to take account of funding. If we adopt these more flexible models outside of the system built on the medical model, what will be the effect on insurance and our definition of it? And we have to question what we are offering and selling. Yes, we offer services publicly and we sell them privately. Capitalism won't go away and should not go away. A balance of public and private models will always be essential.

Europe has interesting models. If we stop fighting over the nonissue of "socialism" we can look at models elsewhere; they are diverse and numerous. It seems that with appropriate government control and moderation, private companies can compete and be profitable while yielding cost-effective and relatively inexpensive services.

The above-mentioned represent just a sampling of issues. Clearly we have our work cut out for us. The models and the ideas are there for examination and to be selected. But we need to get to work.

HUMAN RESOURCES

We can't decide how to utilize our resources without models. Models don't work without people to implement them. Then we have to decide who we are and how we work together.

Psychiatry is the study (science) of treating mental disorders. Clearly there are disorders that belong in this area of specific expertise. Then comes psychology, which is the science of human and animal behavior. Pathology is not implied but not ruled out, and things begin to get a little murky.

Nurses worked with us at a time when their role was being redefined. They were clearly independent practitioners and, even today, they continue to move toward independence as seen in the existence of nurse practitioners, who give primary care. Of course, in the inner city, they brought their valuable medical expertise.

Then we come to social work. Social workers inspired much of the development of our service delivery system. There are various definitions of what social work is, but I like the one proposed by Wright State University which includes "helping individuals, groups or communities enhance or restore their capacity for social functioning..." Looking back at the Baltimore experience, I think this definition comes closest to what we did. Social work also includes community organization, which was a crucial part of our work. Although Caplan came out of the medical profession, his orientation to prevention led us into the social work arena. Social workers came to the work with a pragmatic orientation and a "can do" attitude.

But with new models and applications we also need to consider the paraprofessional community worker. Our experience led us to conclude that they clearly had a place. The idea of "street smarts" was oversold. Yet the people we hired brought with them an understanding of the culture of the population we served and knowledge of the workings of community agencies. Once brought into the professional family, they had the opportunity to develop other sophisticated skills. Many of them proved to have the capacity to develop sound consultation and education skills and some became effective lay therapists.

The idea that the poor in our area could become very useful employees was relatively new. We found the crucial piece was to use a very careful selection process as outlined earlier. Interviewing them was particularly interesting. Some candidates came looking for a job, any job, and were passive, seeming not to be interested in the substance of the job. The good candidates came bright-eyed and inquired about the nature of the job. They made eye contact and asked meaningful questions.

When we first raised the issue of hiring people out of the community some people in the State and the University indicated that they saw our population as uniformly disadvantaged, without skills, hope, or a future. Such a view ignored social reality.

Concerning families where wealth has been accumulated, the saying is, "It takes a generation to make it, a generation to keep it and a generation to lose it." In part this is a reference to one form of the phenomenon of regression toward the mean. In instances where intelligence begins at a high level, intelligence tends to drift down through generations toward average. But among the poor a reverse phenomenon exists. There are notable successes where intelligent and talented people rise from poverty, and we found people with considerable promise. They were effective socially and provided needed services at a lower cost.

And then there is the matter of volunteers. At various times people float the idea of a national volunteer corps of one form or another. Yes, volunteers have real potential but there is a possible group of volunteers beyond a young committed corps who hold considerable promise and they are our retired people. There is a special need attached to them.

There was a time when men retired at age 65 and were, on average, dead by 67. Now we have a growing population of elderly who are healthy. It is a bad idea socially to have millions of people in retirement for 20 or 30 years who make limited or no contribution to the society. Not long ago early retirement was an ideal, but the question always had to be asked, "And then do what?". We should work for a universally accepted ideal for the healthy seniors - that it is time to give back - and then provide options for how it might be done.

One example can be found in my profession. Most of us who have retired have given up our licenses, but there are a lot of things that can be done without a license and with no liability. When I was in private practice I felt there was an hour of time needed for each hour of face-to-face consultation. In our public clinics, volunteer psychologists can review records and summarize them, visit school personnel, and do testing, among other things. We have a tradition of technicians doing testing under the supervision of a psychologist - only this time, the supervision would, in effect, be a collegial consultation with one person assuming the role of supervisor. I'm sure there are many, many other examples.

My misgivings are in the area of turf. Will volunteers be permitted into the system? The volunteer might have difficulty with being seen as unpaid help, or the person he or she is assisting may feel threatened in a variety of ways. My suspicion is that it will be difficult to develop a viable system but in time it can be done.

Considering the use of human resources also requires raising the issue of cost. We will not have huge amounts of grant funds to spend, but broadening the range of models used has the potential to be cost-effective. The inclusion of paraprofessionals, a young corps of volunteers and retired professionals would markedly increase savings.

How we use our human resources is yet another crucial part of the set of issues which need to be evaluated. The application of models depends on how we use these resources. No part of a reformation of the field is independent from another.

PREPARING FOR REFORMATION

Any type of reformation is a long term project that cannot be taken on by one body alone. Including the initial conceptual work, it would need to be broken down into useful components for study and probably pilot studies. And, yes, a crucial piece, which was missing in Baltimore, would need to be included. Evaluation with an open and supportive context would be crucial. New ventures are not born whole and need time to mature, both in the nuts and bolts of operation and in a social sense as acceptance and understanding are built among social animals.

The evaluation of how to proceed would include an understanding of what science and research has told us as well as understanding the evolving social scene. Attention to fostering effective functioning in behalf of the self, family, and society is no small undertaking. And we do need to know to what we are dedicating ourselves.

OPERATIONALIZING THE PROCESS

The list of opportunities, procedures, and possibilities is almost endless. Among them are:

- Commitment to a broader vision
- Evaluation of what research and science in general has taught us
- Adoption of alternative models going well beyond the medical model
- Defining services both preventive and goal directed
- Reevaluation of all human resources including paraprofessionals and volunteers
- Defining ways to support and enhance community members with vision
- Attending to means to foster effective adhocratic functioning rather than bureaucracy
- Making intervention options clear and transparent
- Seeking cost-effective uses for personnel
- Fostering efficiency of procedures, records and prevention

COMMENT

It is important not to look at what happened to the community mental health movement as a failure. It had its own history and flowered in a moment in time. The Poverty Program also virtually disappeared. But both of them left a lasting impression and lessons learned both positive and negative.

The conservative-progressive pendulum was sure to swing, as were economic winds of change and the business cycle. But now, as we recover from the recent recession, we see renewed opportunity and a growing body of knowledge. We do not have to recreate anything. We can take the lessons learned and move forward.

The form of the large commitment to community mental health will not come again, but we learned much and it need not be lost anymore than what we learned in the War on Poverty need be lost.

Being in disarray at the beginning of another reform movement is not a catastrophe. It is an opportunity. The pendulum is still swinging but now in another direction. Are we willing to look at ourselves, take in the information we have and make a commitment in behalf of our society and its well-being?

References and Resources

Burt, Mala, & Roger Burt, *Stepfamilies*: *The Step By Step Model of Brief Therapy* (New York: Brunner/Mazel,1996).

Caplan, Gerald, *Principles of Preventive Psychiatry* (New York: Basic Books, 1964).

Cumming, Elaine, & John Cumming, *Closed Ranks - An Experiment in Mental Health Education* (Cambridge, MA: Harvard University Press, 1957).

Gambone, Michael D., *The Greatest Generation Comes Home* (College Station, TX: Texas A&M University Press, 2005).

Keniston, Kenneth, "*How Community Mental Health Stamped Out the Riots* (1968-1978)", *Trans-action*, July/August 1968.

Riessman, Frank & Arthur Pearl, *New Careers for the Poor* (New York: MacMillan, 1966).

* Note - The primary focus of this book is to provide a retrospective on the experience of a mental health program at the beginning of the community mental health movement, the lessons learned and how those lessons give guidance for the future. A review of the literature was not undertaken. There are many fine books regarding community mental health that have come out since this experience that deserve reading.

Visit www.rogerburt.com for more commentary and comments.

Contact me and send your comments or reviews to
roger.burt@earthlink.net

www.ingramcontent.com/pod-product-compliance
Lightning Source LLC
Chambersburg PA
CBHW022108280326
41933CB00007B/297